# FATE Presents
# UFOs and the ET Presence

Pilot Kenneth Arnold's historic sighting of flying discs near Mt. Rainier, Washington on June 24, 1947 inspired the founding of FATE and graced the cover of the premiere issue, Spring 1948.

**FATE Presents**

# UFOs and the ET Presence

Compiled & Edited by
Rosemary Ellen Guiley

Visionary Living Publishing/Visionary Living, Inc.
New Milford, Connecticut

*FATE Presents: UFOs and the ET Presence*

Compiled and edited by Rosemary Ellen Guiley

Copyright Visionary Living, Inc. 2018

All rights reserved.
No part of this book may be reproduced or
used in any form without permission.

Front cover design by April Slaughter
Back cover and interior design by Leslie McAllister

ISBN: 978-1-942157-33-5 (pbk.)
ISBN: 978-1-942157-34-2 (ebook)

Visionary Living Publishing/Visionary Living, Inc.
New Milford, Connecticut
www.visionarylivingpublishing.com

# Table of Contents

Introduction — ix

## Encounters and Strange Phenomena
I Did See the Flying Disks! · *Kenneth Arnold* — 3
What Were the "Doughnuts"? · *John C. Ross* — 13
The Nazi UFOs · *W.A. Harbinson* — 21
Frank Kaufmann: Roswell Eyewitness? · *Kevin D. Randle* — 31
The Monster and the Saucer · *Gray Barker* — 45
Inside the Flying Saucers... Pancakes · *Paul Foght* — 53
UFOs, Mothman and Me · *John A. Keel* — 59
Russian Submarines and Unidentified Submersible Objects · *Paul Stonehill* — 69
Things That Fall From UFOs · *Ray Palmer* — 77
The Sinister Men in Black · *John A. Keel* — 85

## Abductions
Kidnapped by UFO · *Allen Spraggett* — 97
An Alien Heat: Chronicles of Sex and Saucery · *Scott Corrales* — 107
Alien Abduction Workload · *Robert J. Durant* — 121

## Science, Religion and Metaphysics
Open Letter to Science · *J. Allen Hynek* — 131
Why Science Should Investigate the Evidence for ET Visitation · *Rosemary Ellen Guiley* — 137
An Interview with Dr. Jacques Vallee · *George W. Earley* — 143
On Remote Viewing, UFOs and Extraterrestrials · *Ingo Swann* — 159
Vatican Gives Nod to ETs · *Paola Leopizzi Harris* — 171
The Critters Who Live in Space · *John White* — 179
UFOs, the Universe and Mr. John M. Cage · *James W. Moseley* — 189
Are UFOs Alive? · *Brad Steiger* — 197

**Personalities**

| | |
|---|---|
| The Men Who Ride in Saucers · *Max B. Miller* | 205 |
| George Adamski and the Blustery Day · *Richard W. Heiden* | 213 |
| Long John Nebel: UFO Pitchman · *Timothy Green Beckley* | 217 |

**Perspectives**

| | |
|---|---|
| Fifty Years of UFOs · *The Editors of FATE* | 229 |
| About FATE Magazine | 245 |
| About Rosemary Ellen Guiley | 247 |

# Introduction

FATE owes its very existence to UFOs. The Kenneth Arnold sighting of flying discs over Mt. Rainier, Washington on June 24, 1947 inspired Ray Palmer and Curtis B. Fuller to co-found FATE magazine. The premier issue, Spring 1948, featured the Arnold story on the cover.

Palmer and Fuller were veteran explorers of the unknown, and FATE quickly became established as the go-to magazine for fascinating articles on all things mysterious. Over the decades, FATE has published more articles on UFOs and extraterrestrials than any other topic, but its umbrella stretches far and wide, taking in cryptids, the paranormal and even the spiritual and mystical.

FATE has published more than 730 issues since 1948 and is now under the ownership of Phyllis Galde. The wealth and depth of UFO-related articles are astounding, and one can follow the evolution of ufology through the pages of FATE. Many of the leading names in the field have contributed well-researched articles that hold great historical value today.

As one might imagine, choosing the articles for an anthology is a daunting task – what to leave out is harder to decide than what to include. Fortunately, there will be multiple volumes in the "FATE Presents" series devoted to UFOs. In this first volume, articles span a time frame from the premiere issue to the present. I have given emphasis to the early years of ufology, and have included some of the "classics" – Kenneth Arnold's sighting; famous cases such as Roswell, Flatwoods, Betty and Barney Hill and Mothman; famous personalities such as George Adamski, Long John Nebel and Jacques Vallee; and topical articles by equally famous personalities such as Ingo Swann, Gray Barker, James Moseley, John A. Keel and Timothy Green Beckley.

Readers will especially appreciate "The Men Who Ride in Saucers," a 1960 article by Max B. Miller about a "flying saucer clubs" convention in Los Angeles, written a bit tongue in cheek about some of the colorful presenters and attendees. In some respects, things haven't changed in ufology. Every UFO conference has a fringe component that taxes the boggle points for outsiders and a few insiders as well. However, this is a field of study rife with trickster elements, even more so than the paranormal and cryptozoology. The only rule is there are no rules. Truth is indeed stranger than fiction. Ask any UFO/ET experiencer who has been ridiculed for going public.

In account after account of sightings and encounters over the decades, the response of investigators has been first to ascertain the sanity of the witnesses. There was – and still is – an underlying assumption that people who see UFOs and aliens must be crazy, hallucinating, dreaming, mistaken or up to a hoax. No wonder ufology struggles for credibility, when eyewitness evidence is automatically treated with suspicion.

Readers also will appreciate "Alien Abduction Workload" by Robert J. Durant, who analyzes the mind-boggling numbers of aliens, humans and hours that would have to be involved in abductions, if we are to believe surveys and reports.

John White, in "The Critters Who Live in Space," and Brad Steiger in "Are UFOs Alive?" weigh in on Trevor James Constable's work that UFOs are living beings. They provide thought-provoking material related not only to how we regard UFOs but also to implications for the development of free energy. James W. Moseley's article, "UFOs, The Universe and Mr. John M. Cage," also delves into sentient UFOs.

These are just a few of the 25 substantial articles featured in the book. The material is divided into sections:

**Encounters and Strange Phenomena** features sightings and encounters with craft, aliens and mysterious entities.

**Abductions** features famous alien kidnapping cases.

**Science, Religion and Metaphysics** looks at UFOs from these viewpoints: the failure of science to take ufology seriously; the toe in the water from religious authorities; and the concept that UFOs are not craft but living, sentient beings.

**Personalities** features articles about, and interviews with, celebrities in the field. The interview with Jacques Vallee is especially illuminating.

**Perspectives** is a roundup of leading ufologists discussing the most important events and developments in modern ufology's first 50 years.

## INTRODUCTION

The original FATE publication dates are given at the end of every article, and most also include a short author bio (in some cases, no bio was provided by FATE). FATE has changed its publication schedule and no longer puts a month and year on the issues but uses an issue number instead.

The photos and illustrations come from the pages of FATE as well. In some cases, where photos were printed on newsprint, the images are a bit grainy. Nonetheless, they are the originals that ran with the articles. I have left two different spellings intact in the articles: discs and disks, grays and greys. Some of the artwork are accompanied by their original captions.

UFO/ET researchers and enthusiasts will find this book an invaluable resource. UFO history was recorded by FATE, and now that history is brought to renewed light.

– Rosemary Ellen Guiley, Executive Editor, FATE

# Encounters and Strange Phenomena

# I Did See the Flying Disks!
## Kenneth Arnold

The following story of what I observed over the Cascade Mountains, as impossible as it may seem, is positively true. I never asked nor wanted any notoriety for just accidentally being in the right spot at the right time to observe what I did. I reported something that I know any pilot would have reported. I don't think that in any way my observation was due to sensitivity of eyesight or judgment other than what is considered normal for any pilot.

On Tuesday, June 24th, 1947, I had finished my work for the Central Air Service at Chehalis, Washington, and at about two o'clock I took off from Chehalis, Washington airport with the intention of going to Yakima, Washington. My trip was delayed for an hour to search for a large Marine transport that supposedly went down near or around the southwest side of Mt. Rainier in the state of Washington. (This airplane has been discovered at the time of this writing – July 29, 1947.)

I flew directly toward Mt. Rainier after reaching an altitude of about 9,500 feet, which is the approximate elevation of the high plateau from which Mt. Rainier rises. I had made one sweep of this high plateau to the westward, searching all the various ridges for this Marine ship, and flew to the west down and near the ridge side of the canyon where Ashford, Washington, is located.

Unable to see anything that looked like the lost ship, I made a 360-degree turn to the right and above the little city of Mineral, starting again toward Mt. Rainier. I climbed back up to an altitude of approximately 9,200 feet. I trimmed out my airplane in the direction of Yakima, Washington, which was almost directly east of my position.

The air was so smooth that day that it was a real pleasure flying and, as most pilots do when the air is smooth and they are flying at a higher altitude, I simply sat in my plane observing the sky and terrain.

There was a DC4 to the left and to the rear of me approximately 15 miles distant and, I should judge, at 14,000 feet elevation.

The sky and air were as clear as crystal. I had not flown more than two or three minutes on my course when a bright flash reflected on my airplane. It startled me as I thought I was too close to some other aircraft. I looked every place in the sky and couldn't find where the reflection had come from until I looked to the left and the north of Mt. Rainier, where I observed a chain of nine peculiar-looking aircraft flying from north to south at approximately 9,500 feet elevation and going, seemingly, in a definite direction of about 170 degrees north to south.

They were approaching Mt. Rainier very rapidly, and I merely assumed they were jet planes. Anyhow, I discovered that this was where the reflection had come from, as two or three of them every few seconds would dip or change their course slightly, just enough for the sun to strike them at an angle that reflected brightly in my eyes.

These objects being quite far away, I was unable for a few seconds to make out their shape or their formation. Very shortly they approached Mt. Rainier, and I observed their outline against the snow quite plainly.

I thought it was very peculiar that I couldn't find their tails, but assumed they were some new type of jet. I was determined to clock their speed. I had two definite points – Mt. Rainier and Mt. Adams – to clock them by, and the air was so clear that it was very easy to see the objects and determine their approximate shape and size as far as 50 miles.

I remember distinctly that my sweep-second hand on my eight-day clock, which is located on my instrument panel, read one minute to

## I Did See the Flying Disks!

3 PM as the first object of this formation passed the southern edge of Mt. Rainier. I watched these objects with great interest as I had never before observed airplanes flying so close to the mountaintops, flying directly south to southeast down the hog's back of a mountain range. I would estimate their elevation could have varied a thousand feet one way or another up or down, but they were pretty much on the horizon to me which would indicate they were near the same elevation as I was.

They flew, as I have frequently observed geese fly, in a rather diagonal chainlike line as if they were linked together. They seemed to hold a definite direction but swerved in and out of the high mountain peaks. Their speed at the time did not impress me particularly, because I knew that our army and air forces had planes that went very fast.

What kept bothering me as I watched them flip and flash in the sun right along their path was the fact that I couldn't make out any tail on them, and I am sure that any pilot would justify more than a second look at such a plane.

I observed them quite plainly, and I estimate my distance from them, which was almost at right angles, to be between 20 and 25 miles. I knew they must be very large to permit me to observe their shape at that distance, even as clear a day as it was. In fact, I compared a zeus fastener or cowling tool I had in my pocket with them, holding it up on them and holding it up on the DC4 that I could observe at quite a distance to my left, and they seemed smaller than the DC4; but I should judge their span would have been as wide as the farthest engines on each side of the fuselage of the DC4.

The more I observed these objects, the more upset I became, as I am accustomed to and familiar with most all flying objects whether I am close to the ground or at higher altitudes. I observed the chain of these objects passing another high snow-covered ridge in between Mt. Rainier and Mt. Adams, and as the first one was passing the south crest of this ridge the last object was entering the northern crest of the ridge.

As I was flying in the direction of this particular ridge, I measured it and found it to be approximately five miles, so I could safely assume that the chain of these saucer-like objects was at least five miles long. I could quite accurately determine their pathway due to the fact that there were several of them as well as higher peaks on the other side of their pathway.

As the last unit of this formation passed the northernmost high snow-covered crest of Mt. Adams, I looked at my sweep-second hand and it showed that they had traveled the distance in one minute and 42 seconds. Even at the time this timing did not upset me as I felt confident that after I landed there would be some explanation of what I had seen.

A number of newsmen and experts suggested that I might have been seeing reflections or even a mirage. This I know to be absolutely false, as I observed these objects not only through the glass of my airplane but turned my airplane sideways where I could open my window and observe them with a completely unobstructed view.

Even though two minutes seems like a very short time to one on the ground, in the air in two minutes' time a pilot can observe a great many things and anything within his field of vision probably as many as 50 or 60 times.

I continued my search for the Marine plane, for another 15 or 20 minutes, and while searching for this Marine plane the things I had just observed kept going through my mind. I became more disturbed, so after taking a last look at Teton Reservoir I headed for Yakima.

I might add that my complete observation of these objects, which I could even follow by their flashes as they passed Mt. Adams, was around two and one-half or three minutes – although by the time they reached Mt. Adams they were out of my range of vision as far as determining shape or form. Of course, when the sun reflected from one or two or three of these units, they appeared to be completely round; but, I am making a drawing to the best of my ability, which I am including, as to the shape I observed these objects to be as they passed the snow-covered ridges at Mt. Rainier.

When these objects were flying approximately straight and level, they were just a thin black line and the only time I could get a judgment as to their size was when they flipped.

These objects were holding an almost constant elevation; they did not seem to be going up or to be coming down, such as would be the case of rockets or artillery shells. I am convinced in my own mind that they were some type of airplane, even though they did not conform with the many aspects of the conventional type of planes that I know.

Although these objects have been reported by many other observers throughout the United States, there have been six or seven other

*Kenneth Arnold and his Callair airplane on the day after his historic sighting.*

accounts written by some of these observers that I can truthfully say must have observed the same thing that I did; particularly, the descriptions of the three Western Air Lines employees of Cedar City, Utah; the pilot from Oklahoma City; the locomotive engineer in Illinois, John Corlett; a United Press correspondent of Boise, Idaho; Dave Johnson, news editor at the *Boise Daily Statesman;* Captain Smith, a copilot; Stevens and Marty Morrow of United Air Lines; and Captain Charles F. Gebian and Jack Harvey of United Air Lines, both of whom on July 28, 1947 made their observation on United Air Lines flight 105 westbound out of Boise.

It is my opinion that descriptions could not be very accurate taken from the ground unless these saucer-like discs were at quite a great height, and there is a possibility that all of the people who observed peculiar objects could have seen the same thing I did; but, it would have been very difficult from the ground to observe these for more than four or five seconds, and there is always the possibility of atmospheric moisture and dust near the ground which could distort one's vision, while air observers I would judge to be much more accurate.

I have in my possession letters from all over the United States and Europe from people who profess that these objects have been observed over other portions of the world, principally Sweden, Bermuda and California.

I would have given almost anything that day to have had a movie camera with a telephoto lens and from now on I will never be without one.

When I landed at Yakima, Washington airport I described what I had seen to my very good friend, Al Baxter, who is the General Manager of Central Aircraft Company. He listened patiently and was very courteous but in a joking way didn't believe me.

I did not accurately measure the distance between these two mountains until I landed at Pendleton, Oregon that same day. I told a number of pilot friends what I had observed, and they did not scoff or laugh, but suggested they might be guided missiles or something new. In fact, several former Army pilots informed me that they had been briefed before going into combat overseas that they might see objects of similar shape and design that I described and assured me that I wasn't dreaming or going crazy. I quote Sonny Robinson, a former Army Air Force pilot who is now operating dusting operations at Pendleton, Oregon: "What you observed, I am convinced, is some type of jet or rocket-propelled

*Kenneth Arnold and his wife, Doris, with the Callair.*

ship that is in the process of being tested by our government or it could even be by some foreign government."

Anyhow, the news that I had observed these spread very rapidly and before the night was over I was receiving telephone calls from all parts of the world; and to date I have not received one telephone call or one letter of scoffing or disbelief. The only disbelief that I know of was what was printed in the papers. I look at this whole affair as not something funny as some people have made it out to be. To me it is mighty serious and since I evidently did observe something that at least Mr. John Doe on the street corner or Pete Andrews on the ranch has never heard about, is no reason that it does not exist.

Even though I openly invited an investigation by the Army and the FBI as to the authenticity of my story or a mental and physical examination as to my capabilities, I received no interest from these two important protective forces of our country until two weeks after my observation. I will go so far as to assume that if our military intelligence was not aware of what I observed and reported to the United [Press International] and Associated Press and over the radio on two different occasions which apparently set the nation buzzing, they would be the very first people I could expect as visitors.

*Arnold's sighting near Mt. Rainier. Painting by Mike Boss.*

I have received lots of requests from people who told me to make a lot of wild guesses. I have based what I have written here in this article on positive facts and as far as guessing what it was I observed, it is just as much a mystery to me as it is to the rest of the world. I saw them and I know they are real.

My pilot's license is 33489. I fly a Callair airplane, which is a three-place single-engine land ship that is designed and manufactured at Afton, Wyoming, as an extremely high-performance, high-altitude airplane that was made for mountain work. The national certificate of my plane is NC33355.

*Kenneth Arnold was born March 29, 1915, in Sebeka, MN. Educated at Minot, ND. Interested in athletics, he was all-state end in 1932-33; a knee injury ended his football career. He worked for Red Comet, Inc., manufacturers of automatic firefighting apparatuses. In 1940 he established his own fire control supply company, the Great Western Fire Control Supply, which handled, distributed and installed firefighting equipment in five states. Arnold died on January 16, 1984 at age 68.*

FATE Spring 1948

# What Were the "Doughnuts"?

## John C. Ross

When I heard the report about the "flying doughnuts" seen by Kenneth Arnold, I had just returned to Chicago from a tour of military research bases on the West Coast, including the Navy's guided missile research center at Point Mugu and the Army's great testing center at Muroc. At these two highly restricted locations I saw plenty, but I did not see anything remotely resembling a "flying doughnut" in configuration or performance.

In fact, I can state quiet flatly that I do not believe there exists in our aircraft companies, in our Army or Navy, or even in the guarded research precincts of NACA any aircraft using the principles of aerodynamics which has ever attained speeds of 1,200 miles per hour – or even the much lower speed of sound – 760 miles per hour at sea level.

I do not believe, furthermore, that we have any power plant capable of propelling any aircraft at such speeds!

I do not pretend to know everything our researchers are doing, but I keep fairly well abreast of what is going on, since I make my living by writing about it. Editors of some of the largest magazines in the country think enough of my knowledge to publish my articles regularly.

We have missiles that attain speeds beyond anything Kenneth Arnold witnessed. These range from rocket propelled ordnance rockets like the bazooka, which uses a single web powder grain, right up to the German V2 with its lox and alcohol and 3,000-miles-an-hour speeds.

Chance-Vought resembles a "saucer" in configuration, but it is slow and only one has been built.

But we do not have anything, missiles included, which could perform as Kenneth Arnold saw these "doughnuts" perform. We have no missiles, for instance, which are capable of level flight over the distance that Kenneth Arnold clocked these "flying doughnuts" in level flight. That includes the V2.

We have no missiles, furthermore, which could be launched in train and which would keep in the close formation which Kenneth Arnold reports he saw these "flying doughnuts." We do have missiles and aircraft which approach a doughnut roughly in shape, but these are pilot

## What Were the "Doughnuts"?

orders only; they simply do not exist in even the small numbers that Kenneth Arnold saw them. I'll go into this in some detail a little later on.

Now as a science writer, knowing what I know about aerodynamics, about the terrific barriers which still must be overcome before we exceed the speed of sound in any aircraft using wings for lift, and about research developments in general, I could say that Kenneth Arnold did not see the "flying doughnuts" at all.

But that would be the easy way out. All I am prepared to say about this now is that if Kenneth Arnold really did see the "flying doughnuts," and if they performed as he said they did, I do not believe they were manufactured in the United States or in the Soviet Union or even on Planet Earth itself.

I realize that my neck is out a foot when I write this. But I am convinced that I do know enough about late developments to warrant my statements.

Even if I did not, I know enough about aerodynamics generally to know that we are still so far from reaching supersonic speeds in our airplanes that even if my specific knowledge on late types should be faulty, my general knowledge isn't.

We just don't have supersonic aircraft and neither does Russia nor any other country.

We do not have them either in configuration or in power plant. We do not even have supersonic wind tunnels of sufficient size to provide us with the basic research data we still need.

I have seen some very advanced planes, both on the ground and in flight. These include two models of the rocket-propelled Bell XS1 and the tiny-winged Douglas D588, a transonic jet airplane.

The Army and Navy are very hush-hush about these planes, but my personal opinion is that neither one has yet flown as fast as 700 miles an hour, which is only half that of the clocked speed of the "flying doughnuts."

Our knowledge of aircraft, in short, comes up against some very practical barriers. We can achieve supersonic speeds with long slim rocket-like configurations. We can launch such craft very well, but we can never land them without wings. And we have no winged craft that at the present time can fly faster than sound!

I am familiar with three aircraft (plus their modifications) that might be mistaken for doughnut-shaped craft at a distance. I will describe them here and explain why I do not believe they were the craft that Kenneth Arnold saw. So far as I know, there are no other planes that even remotely resemble a doughnut in configuration.

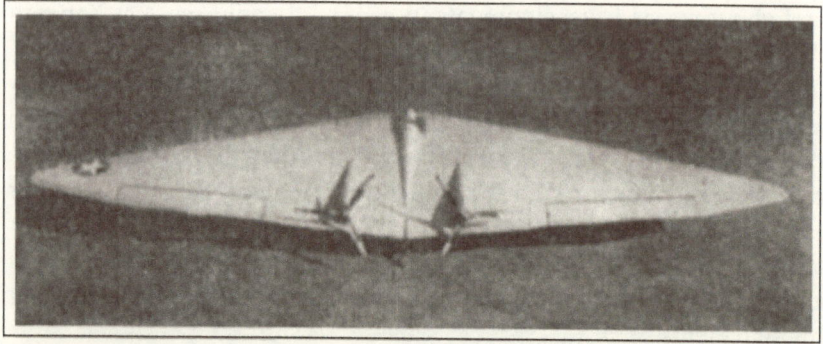

*Northrop N1M is typical of experimental wings that resemble Arnold's saucers, but all are far too slow.*

*Northrop XB-35 is the only flying wing as large as Arnold reported saucers to be. Several of these have been built, including the similar jet-propelled XB-49, but they do not begin to have the performance he estimates for the flying disks.*

## What Were the "Doughnuts"?

First of these are the flying wing planes made by Northrop. These include a great many experimental craft such as the N1M, N9M, the MX324 and the XP79 (Flying Ram). These were all small planes and the first two were built to develop flying characteristics of the later B35 and B49.

I have seen most of these, and although they are closer to doughnut shapes than conventional planes, because of their big broad wings and lack of tails, they really do not resemble doughnuts. They do not have the speed of the "flying doughnuts" and they have not been built in large enough numbers so that nine of them could be assembled and flown in formation.

Only four N9Ms were built, for instance. They carried one person and had a 60-foot wingspan. They were designed to train pilots for the big B35s and to test the B35 design. In flight they look more like giant manta rays than anything else I can think of.

This same general proposition holds for the N1M, an earlier model, and all the various versions and modifications of these planes. They were all propeller driven, which automatically limits them to subsonic speed ranges.

The XP79 Flying Ram was jet driven and had speeds of over 500 miles an hour, but it had much the same configuration. The earlier MX324 was rocket driven but was not exactly successful because the rocket motors did not develop enough thrust.

The big flying wings – B35 and B49 – also follow the general Northrop wing configurations. They differ from the others mainly in size. The former is propeller driven, the latter is propelled by the jet method and has recently taken its test flights. Although the B35 is understood to be on a production basis, not enough of them have been built to make it possible to assemble a formation – and indeed as this is written they had attained total flight time all told of less than 100 hours.

Much closer in shape to a doughnut are the two Vought planes, the prototype V173 and the later XF5U1. These planes actually look like great flat beetles, with the nacelles of the remotely driven propellers protruding like giant crab eyes on a stalk. The highest speed yet announced for the XF5U1 is 425 miles per hour, and even if it can go a great deal faster its speed would still be sharply limited by the fact that it is a propeller driven craft. On the other hand, if jet engines should be installed, it undoubtedly would become much faster – yet still in the subsonic range.

*German-designed Jaeger P-13 could acheive speed claimed for flying saucers but it is believed the model never got beyond experimental stage.*

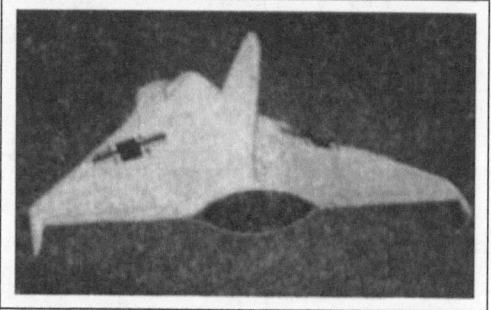

*Another view of P-13 shows orifice of ram jet engine. All-wing craft was designed for speeds of 1,500 mph.*

The Jaeger P13 looks even more like a manta ray than the Northrop flying wings. The Jaeger P13 was designed by the German scientist Alexander Lippisch who is now understood to be in this country, and who also designed the German rocket plane, the Me163.

The Jaeger P13 was intended to fly at 1,500 miles per hour, although one American scientist estimated it might do 2,200 miles per hour. It was powered with a ram jet engine which has no moving parts. The air simply enters the front of the engine, where it is rammed into the combustion chamber by the high speed of the craft itself. In the combustion chamber it is mixed with fuel and ignited, blasting out the rear. The ram jet can operate in the atmosphere but not in space. And it is not theory – it actually works and a great deal of research is underway on it. The P13 also had the sharply sweptback wings of a supersonic craft and undoubtedly would have met the performance goals of its German designers.

There is only one trouble with identifying this craft as a "flying doughnut." So far as is known, no P13 ever flew; it is believed that no full-scale model was ever completed. A prototype was under construction when the war ended, however, and it is quite possible that the Americans taking over might have completed it.

But that is a long way from producing nine such planes and having them far enough advanced to fly in formation as of June 24, 1947. First, the ram jet engines probably are not far enough advanced. Second, the sharply sweptback wings of this revolutionary design, and other design features, result in a plane that is extremely difficult to keep under control in the air. It would be bound to be unstable, and it is likely that many more years of research would be necessary to knock the bugs out of the design.

Lastly, of course, this plane does not really look very much like a flying doughnut. It is, however, the only design we have even considered here which might achieve the performance of the craft that Kenneth Arnold saw. It, or something very like it, is the only one of the three that I would not rule out as being a possibility – even though as far as I know it has never flown.

Where do we stand then?

I have heard it suggested that the planes were either Army or Navy craft of extremely secret design. Since we are not at war, the air forces could not suppress news about these craft having been seen. And since they do not want to admit they are in development, they just play dumb about it . . .

You have probably heard the above hypothesis. I think that this article has proved it wrong.

Last, I have heard it asked, "What were these planes doing out there anyway?"

You have me there.

If you want my candid personal opinion, it is that Mr. Arnold either saw a mirage or he did not see anything at all.

But if he did see what he describes, it was a train of space ships from some other planet!

FATE Spring 1948

# The Nazi UFOs

## W.A. Harbinson

The Nazi connection with regard to UFOs, originally flying saucers, can be said to have begun in 1944, toward the end of World War II, when various Allied pilots reported being harassed during their bombing raids by unidentified flying objects, soon nicknamed "foo fighters," that were described variously as "red balls of fire that flew off the aircraft's wing tips, other balls of fire that flew in front of them" and "lights which appear off in the distance – like a Christmas tree in the air – and flicker on and off."

According to the reports of Allied pilots, the foo fighters climbed, descended or turned when the Allied aircraft did – and also flew away when fired upon. Other official reports recorded that the foo fighters flew in parallel formation with the Allied aircraft, often pacing them for great distances, at speeds exceeding 300 mph, frequently causing their engines to malfunction by cutting in and out. This soon led to speculation that the foo fighters were German secret weapons, radio-controlled from the ground, and designed either to foul the ignition systems of the bombers or to act as psychological weapons that confused and unnerved the Allied pilots.

Sightings of the foo fighters tailed off and then ceased completely a few weeks before the end of the war.

Renato Vesco was an aircraft engineer specializing in aerospace and ramjet developments. Educated before World War II at the University of Rome, he then studied aeronautical engineering at the German Institute for Aerial Development. During the war, he was sent to work with the Germans at Fiat's immense underground installations at Lake Garda, near Limone in northern Italy, where he helped in the production of various aeronautical devices that were tested in great secrecy at the Hermann Goering Institute of Riva del Garda. After the war, in the 1960s, Vesco worked for the Italian Air Ministry of Defense as an undercover technical agent, tasked with investigating the UFO phenomenon.

According to Vesco, captured German scientific papers indicated that by 1945 the Nazi research centers of Volkenrode and Guidonia were working on a revolutionary new type of aircraft that was devoid of all surface protuberances, such as wings and rudders, devoid even of normal air intakes, and powered by a highly advanced turbine engine. This was in fact the so-called "foo fighter" – actually the German Feuerball, or Fireball, which, though evolved from the research work done at Volkenrode and Guidonia, was constructed at an aeronautical establishment at Wiener Neustadt, Austria.

The Feuerball was a relatively small, armor-plated, disc-shaped antiradar device powered by a special turbojet engine. It was radio-controlled at the moment of takeoff, but then, attracted by the enemy (Allied) aircraft's exhaust fumes, it automatically followed that aircraft, automatically avoided colliding with it, and automatically short-circuited the aircraft's radar and ignition systems. During the day, this device looked exactly like "a shining disc spinning on its axis" and by night it looked like a "burning globe."

Vesco also claimed that the basic principles of the Nazis' Feuerball were later applied to a much larger symmetrical circular aircraft, the Kugelblitz, or Ball Lightning Fighter, which was the first example of the vertical-rising, jet-lift aircraft.

Among all the nations of Earth, Germany was the one most obsessed with the development of vertical-rising, saucer-shaped aircraft. German scientists and engineers believed that the perfect flying machine would be one that required no runway, since it would take off

*Depiction of a possible Nazi UFO-shaped craft.*

vertically, would be able to hover in midair, and would not be limited in maneuverability or speed by the "boundary layer" first discovered by the renowned physicist, Professor Ludwig Prandtl, in 1904. As the buildup of the boundary layer is dramatically increased by the many surface protuberances of a normal aircraft – wings, tails, rudders, rotors and cockpits – it was felt that by getting rid of them completely, by somehow wrapping them together as part and parcel of the one, circular, smooth-surfaced flying wing, the first step in the conquest of the boundary layer would be achieved.

Germany was the country with most interest in such developments and certainly the most advanced at that time. A disc- or saucer-shaped aircraft, without any surface protuberances, powered by ultra-high-speed engines, is what they were after, and many designs of the time were based on that conception. It is therefore no accident that as early as 1935 a German, Hans von Ohain, had applied for a patent for a jet engine. Nor was it an accident that the first flight of a jet-powered aircraft was made by a Heinkel He178 at Rostock, Germany, on August 27, 1939.

Regarding vertical-rising aircraft, the Focke-Achgelis Company had already announced in 1939 that it had almost completed its FW61 helicopter, which would be the first fully operational helicopter in existence. That the Germans produced the first successful helicopter yet were not known to have used such craft during World War II, may be due to the fact that already they were more concerned with tailless aircraft, or "flying wings," devoid of vertical stabilizing or control surfaces. This would lead them to the search for a jet-propelled, disc-shaped aircraft, or flying saucer.

At the end of World War II, Germany's scientific papers had been hidden, and were eventually found, in tunnels, caves, dry wells, ploughed fields, river beds and even cesspits. Also found the length and breadth of Nazi Germany were the well-known V1 flying bombs and V2 rockets, as well as lesser known, but equally formidable, heat-guided ground-to-air missiles, sonic guidance torpedoes, the highly advanced UXXI and UXXIII electrical submarines, ME262 jetfighters, rocket planes that flew even faster than the Messerschmitts, the prototypes for other, vertical-rising jet aircraft, the beginnings of an atom bomb project, and even, in the immense, underground Riva del Garda complex, where Renato Vesco had worked, the manufacturing process for a metallic material which could withstand temperatures of about 1000 degrees Centigrade.

Even more important was the discovery of various porous metals or aero-permeable surfaces that had been created by the scientists of Göttingen, Aachen, and Volkenrode – various compounds of magnesium and aluminum, sinterized and permeated with microscopic holes. Known as Luftschwamm, or "aerosponge," this was exactly the kind of metal that the British aerodynamics expert, Professor E. F. Relf, had said could create "frictionless airflow" and enable an aircraft to slip through the air in the same way as a piece of wet soap slips through the fingers. The speed and maneuvering capabilities of such a craft would be virtually limitless.

*Top view of possible Nazi UFO-shaped craft.*

## Thule

Parallel with these scientific developments was the Nazis' growing obsession with the creation of a master-and-slave society, the masters being fanatical members of Heinrich Himmler's Death's Head SS, the slaves being former concentration camp inmates and people abducted from all over conquered Europe. Hitler and Himmler both believed passionately in the historical existence of Thule, presumed to lie off the coast of Greenland.

According to legend, Thule was a long-vanished civilization, like Atlantis, consisting of a pure Aryan or Nordic peoples. In the minds of the more mystically inclined Nazis, who also believed in unorthodox cosmologist Hans Hörbiger's bizarre World Ice theory, this vision of a pure Aryan race, or Master Race, became inextricably entwined with the belief that the lost Thule was not the Thule located in Greenland, but another place altogether: a world of ice and snow. Because of this, Hitler and Himmler began thinking of the resurrection of the Master Race in terms of isolated colonies located in Nordic, or icy, areas where the impurities of German youth could be bred out and the pure Aryan

Master Race be repeated through a process of selective breeding and monastic, military discipline. In pursuit of this ambition, they began looking hopefully to Antarctica.

This much is known. Toward the end of 1938, Hitler sent an expedition commanded by Captain Alfred Richter to the South Atlantic Ocean coastal region of Antarctica. The expedition arrived there in 1939. Daily for three weeks two seaplanes were catapulted from the deck of the German aircraft carrier, *Schwabenland,* with orders to fly back and forth across the territory that previous Norwegian explorers had named Queen Maud Land. According to the *Encyclopaedia Britannica:* "The German Antarctic Expedition of 1939 aerially photographed an extensive segment of the Princess Astrid and Princess Martha coasts of western Queen Maud Land and, dropping metal swastikas over the region, claimed it for the Hitler government. The Germans called this territory Neu Schwabenland."

Throughout the war, German ships and U-boats continued to prowl the South Atlantic Ocean along the coastline of Antarctica, thus blocking any Allied incursions into Neu Schwabenland. They continued to prowl the Antarctic shores until the end of the war.

During the immediate postwar years, there was growing concern among Western intelligence agencies that a great number of high-ranking Nazi officers were covertly traveling to Argentina and from there being flown on to a secret base possibly located in Queen Maud Land, or Neu Schwabenland, in Antarctica. Perhaps impelled by this belief, the Americans, on August 26, 1946, launched the biggest Antarctic expedition in history, Operation Highjump, led by the renowned US explorer and naval officer, Rear Admiral Richard E. Byrd. As Byrd's resources included 13 ships, at least two seaplane tenders, an aircraft carrier, six two-engine R4D transports, six Martin PBM flying boats, six helicopters, and a staggering total of 4,000 men, it was widely believed that the expedition was designed more as an assault force than as a simple exploratory expedition.

It also seemed odd that when this virtual assault force reached the Antarctic coast, it was not only docked, on January 12, 1947, near the German-claimed territory of Neu Schwabenland, but was then divided up into three separate task forces. When the expedition ended, in February the same year, reportedly much earlier than anticipated, there were numerous stories in the press about Rear Admiral Byrd's references to "enemy fighters which came from the polar regions" and could "fly from one pole to the other with incredible speed." The United States then withdrew from Antarctica for a whole decade.

Mere months after Rear Admiral Byrd's Antarctic task force was seemingly routed by enemy fighters which came from the polar regions and could fly from one pole to the other with incredible speed, the first postwar "flying saucer" sightings were reported.

On June 21, 1947, a harbor patrolman, Harold Dahl, accompanied by his 15-year-old son and two crewmen, on harbor patrol near Maury Island in Puget Sound, off Tacoma, Washington, reported seeing six objects shaped like "inflated inner tubes" hovering about 2,000 feet above his boat. The objects were described as being about 100 feet in diameter, metallic, with no jets, rockets, wings or propellers, but with a hole in their center, or base, symmetrically placed portholes around their perimeters, and observatory windows on their undersides.

Three days later, on June 24, an American businessman, Kenneth Arnold, reported that when flying his private Piper Club aeroplane near Mount Rainier in the Cascades, Washington, he had observed nine disc-shaped, apparently metallic objects flying in "a diagonal chainlike line" and making an undulating motion "like a saucer skipping over water."

The term "flying saucer" came into being.

During the months that followed, the United States was plagued by numerous flying saucer sightings, most reported by trained technicians and pilots because the UFOs were appearing increasingly over super-secret military bases. In July 1952, these extraordinary sightings culminated in a massive UFO "invasion" of Washington DC, in which hundreds of UFOs, confirmed by radar operatives as "solid, metallic objects," literally surrounded the capital and even flew through the prohibited corridor above the White House. A similar, equally spectacular, UFO invasion of Washington DC took place a week later. This led to a growing fear in intelligence circles that the men and materials deported from Nazi Germany after the war had led to a dangerous Soviet lead in space technology.

## Designed a flying top?

However, that same year, in a series of interviews given to the West German press, a former Luftwaffe engineer, Flugkapitän Rudolph

Schriever, then resident in Bremerhaven Lehe, West Germany, claimed that during the war he had helped design a vertical-rising "flying top" with an "arched, domed and rounded" pilot's cabin in the center of multiple, circular adjustable jets that were driven by a turbine engine, also located in the center of gravity, under the capsule containing the pilot's cabin. The research program was known as "Projekt Saucer."

The first prototype was successfully test-flown on June 1, 1942, then work began on a larger prototype 2, followed, in 1944, by a third, even larger, prototype 3. Schriever claimed that his final flying disc had been ready for testing at the BMW plant in Prague in early 1944, but with the advance of the Allies into Germany, the test had been cancelled, the machine destroyed to keep it from falling into the hands of the enemy, and his designs either mislaid or stolen. Schriever then fled to the west, reached the American lines, and eventually made it back home to Bremerhaven.

According to Schriever, the other members of the Projekt Saucer team were Walter Miethe, an engineer from the V1 and V2 programs, Klaus Habermohl, another aeronautical engineer, and Dr. Giuseppe Belluzzo from the Riva del Garda complex. This is of particular interest in that while Dr. Belluzzo disappeared at the end of the war and was never heard from again, Klaus Habermohl was captured by the Russians and taken back with them to Russia to work, alongside other captured engineers and rocket scientists, with the notes and materials found in the defeated Nazi Germany. The other Projekt Saucer engineer, Walter Miethe, was similarly taken to America to work under Werner von Braun at the United States' first rocket center in the White Sands Proving Ground, New Mexico. He eventually joined the A.V. Roe (AVRO Canada) aircraft company in Malton, Ontario, reportedly to continue work on disc-shaped aircraft, or flying saucers – just as Habermohl was thought to be doing with the Russians.

There can now be little doubt that the major world powers are working on a wide variety of black technology projects based on the original flying saucer designs of Nazi Germany, and are possibly still developing highly advanced aircraft in more radical configurations in a secret colony in Antarctica, well-hidden and protected by the snow and ice-capped mountain ranges of Neu Schwabenland. If this be the case, they will surely be doing so with the complicity of the numerous

*Depiction of possible Nazi UFO-shaped craft hovering over submarines.*

international research stations now scattered across Antarctica and surrounding Neu Schwabenland.

As far back as 1953, the April edition of the *Royal Air Force Review* stated that it was common knowledge that aircraft designers throughout the world were devoting increasing attention to flying saucers when considering speeds of more than twice that of sound. It also contained a short report about manmade flying saucers that had recently skimmed over the rooftops of Belgrade, Yugoslavia. Reportedly, these were experimental models made by the Yugoslavian Air Force. They were less than 12 inches in diameter, weighed just over four pounds, had a top speed of 31 mph, and were controlled by radio – crude versions of Nazi Germany's more sophisticated antiradar device, the Feuerball.

The influence of former Projekt Saucer engineers like Walter Miethe, who went on to work for the A.V. Roe (AVRO Canada) aircraft company in Malton, Ontario, almost certainly had a bearing on that company's production of two flying saucer prototypes: the Flying Flapjack and the Avrocar, both photographed and widely publicized in 1961. The highly regarded English aeronautical engineer, John Frost, also worked on an AVRO Canada flying saucer prototype that was envisaged to be capable of either hovering virtually motionless in midair or flying at a speed of nearly 2,000 mph and, perhaps more pertinently, was ideal for "subarctic and polar regions."

## The Antarctic?

Given that thousands of people have claimed to have been abducted temporarily by flying saucers for often painful medical examinations by robotic or cyborg-styled crew members, and that over the years thousands of people have inexplicably disappeared from the face of the Earth, never to return, we are left with the chilling possibility that even if they are no longer practicing Nazis, a hidden colony of scientifically minded men and women, living in a master-and-slave society, have taken root in Neu Schwabenland, Antarctica, and are continuing to explore the far reaches of aeronautical, scientific and surgical experimentation unrestricted by the moral qualms of normal societies.

The case remains open.

*W.A. Harbinson: Author of the bestselling UFO epic,* Genesis, *the seminal nonfiction work,* Projekt UFO: The Case for Man-Made Flying Saucers, *and the fact-based novel,* The Wilson Papers.

FATE No. 732

# Frank Kaufmann: Roswell Eyewitness?

## Kevin D. Randle

Frank Kaufmann, one of the most controversial of the Roswell UFO crash figures, died in February 2001, leaving many questions unanswered. If what he said was true, then any explanation for the Roswell UFO crash, other than the extraterrestrial, vanishes. His firsthand observations of the craft, of the bodies, and of the extraordinary efforts by the military to hide the facts leaves no other explanation. That is, of course, if he was telling us the truth.

Kaufmann was originally from New York and had studied art there before the Second World War dragged him to New Mexico. He was an accomplished artist, and his many paintings hung throughout his house. They ranged from landscapes to still life to a few portraits. To my admittedly unskilled eye, they reflected a very talented man.

### Kaufmann's military career

During World War II, Kaufmann served in the Army Air Force as an enlisted man. He rose to master sergeant, according to what he told me,

*Frank J. Kaufmann (1916-2001).*

and he never suggested that he had held a commission. He hinted that he was involved in some sort of intelligence work, though this was never fully explained. He talked of Soviet spies coming up through Mexico, of the Norden bombsight that was so important for the war in Europe and chasing intruders off what was then the Roswell Army Air Field and later Walker Air Force Base.

He mentioned his association with Brigadier General Martin F. Scanlon, who did have an association with intelligence work. Prior to the war, Scanlon had been an attaché to the American embassy in London, whose job it was to spy on German attempts to rebuild their air force. Scanlon was called back to the United States, where Hap Arnold, who was commanding the Army Air Force, asked him to help establish what would become, much later, Air Force intelligence.

These links, between Scanlon and intelligence, and between Scanlon and Kaufmann, provided some measure of validity to the things Kaufmann said much later. Kaufmann knew Scanlon, who had served at Roswell, and he was well aware of Scanlon's intelligence work.

After the war, when the size of the military was being reduced, Kaufmann remained in place in Roswell. He was, however, discharged from the Army and apparently hired by the Army as a civilian, doing the same job he had done before his discharge. This, according to the available records, was as a clerk in the personnel office. According to the documents, he left active service on November 7, 1945, and left his civilian job at the base on December 12, 1947. He quit to take a new and, I would assume, a better job in Roswell.

## There at the retrieval

All of this would be unimportant to us if Kaufmann hadn't said that he was involved in the retrieval of an alien craft in July 1947. I learned that he might have something to do with the case from Walter Haut. Although I don't remember the exact words, Haut said that Frank Kaufmann might be a man to talk to.

I called him on January 4, 1990 and conducted what was probably the very first interview that Kaufmann granted. He was, as always, somewhat reluctant to provide information and answered some of the questions with what would eventually become his stock answer when he didn't like a question: "Well, I don't know."

He told me that he had been assigned to the Roswell base in January 1942 and remained there throughout the war. He said, "I was essentially separated in 1945. Then I was frozen for two years. So, I was out there [at the base] as a civilian for two years."

During this interview, Kaufmann first mentioned Robert Thomas, who supposedly knew something about the UFO crash. Kaufmann told me then that Thomas had been a warrant officer. Later, Kaufmann would suggest that Thomas was actually a brigadier general masquerading as a warrant officer because Thomas didn't want to draw attention to himself.

When I asked about a military assignment for Thomas, Kaufmann said, "He had something to do with security ... top echelon security. When they took, when they found a lot of this equipment ... everything had to be cleared through him first."

## Unsolved mysteries

Kaufmann and I talked for a few more minutes. Now, reading over the transcript of that first conversation, I can see that I provided hints of what I was looking for, and Kaufmann, sharp as he was, certainly would have picked up on those hints. He also pointed out, as we talked, that he had seen the *Unsolved Mysteries* episode that dealt with the Roswell UFO crash. He also hinted that he had discussed this with Walter Haut. If he needed priming for his story, that certainly would have provided more than enough information.

But there is an interesting note. Kaufmann, talking about the show, said, "There was one thing that came to mind as I watched that program." He then explained that he didn't like the scene in which Jesse Marcel, Sr., after collecting debris on the Brazel (Foster) ranch, returned home with it so he could show it to his wife and son.

I suggested that it wasn't actually classified at that point, but Kaufmann said, "It was classified." That told me something about Kaufmann. At the very least, he understood how these things were supposed to work rather than how civilians believed them to work. Officers did not share classified material with family and friends.

I also pointed out that Marcel had known that the debris was not made on Earth. Kaufmann asked, "How would he know?"

These were a couple of things that bothered Kaufmann. He played the whole thing close to the vest, giving little in the way of information – mainly, I believe, because he didn't know who I was or why I was asking the questions.

That was Frank Kaufmann, however. Hinting that he might know something more than the rest of us, hinting that he was on the inside, but never quite confirming it. I should also point out that in this conversation, Kaufmann told me that he had been an enlisted man and that he had been a civilian employee of the government at the time of the crash. It was only later that some would say that Kaufmann had been an officer, that he had been a colonel in intelligence, but he never mentioned anything like that to me and I don't know where those ideas originated.

I met Frank Kaufmann in person not long after that, on Super Bowl weekend, 1990. We – Don Schmitt and I – visited him at his home in Roswell. We sat in the living room and discussed the case to some extent. He then walked us around, showing us his paintings. They filled the walls of most of the rooms.

## The visit with Kaufmann

There was one painting that he seemed to be very fond of. It was mostly reds and browns, showing large trees late in the year, with a strange, grayish face superimposed on the trunk of one of the trees. I thought it looked more like an elf than anything extraterrestrial. It was a very strange painting, and I mention it here only because Kaufmann showed us the painting only two weeks after I first spoke to him, but the picture looked as if it had been painted a long time before that. Later, he would hint that the face resembled those of the alien creatures he had seen in July 1947.

After that, whenever I made it into Roswell, I would call Kaufmann and we would go to breakfast, usually to the Roswell Inn. He would slowly provide information about his involvement at these meetings. Finally, I asked if we could videotape one of the meetings, and he agreed. We sat in his backyard and discussed the Roswell case, with him on one side of the table and Schmitt and I on the other.

## Evolving story

Kaufmann's story evolved over time. Finally, he said that he had been involved from the beginning, that he had been called by Brigadier General Scanlon and asked to drive over to the White Sands Proving Grounds (now the White Sands Missile Range) and see what they had on radar. Kaufmann said that they watched something flit around the sky periodically, but that radar coverage wasn't all that great given both the capabilities of the radar and the mountainous local terrain.

Kaufmann said that they stayed in the radar room for 24 hours, arranging a signal with the operator so that they could go outside or to the latrine. This radar watch, according to Kaufmann, was called off, and he returned to Roswell. Within 24 hours or so, the object was down. Kaufmann said that the radar screen lighted as the craft exploded. Some experts said that a bursting of the craft would not have been reflected on the radar, but there are two ways to explain it. One, when the craft exploded, it sent out a burst of electromagnetic radiation on the same frequency as that used by the radar. The set, reading that burst as a return, would display it in a bright blob of light. Since this was a burst, the signal would fade and the image on the screen would fade. Transponders in commercial airliners can paint the screen in a similar fashion, if the pilot

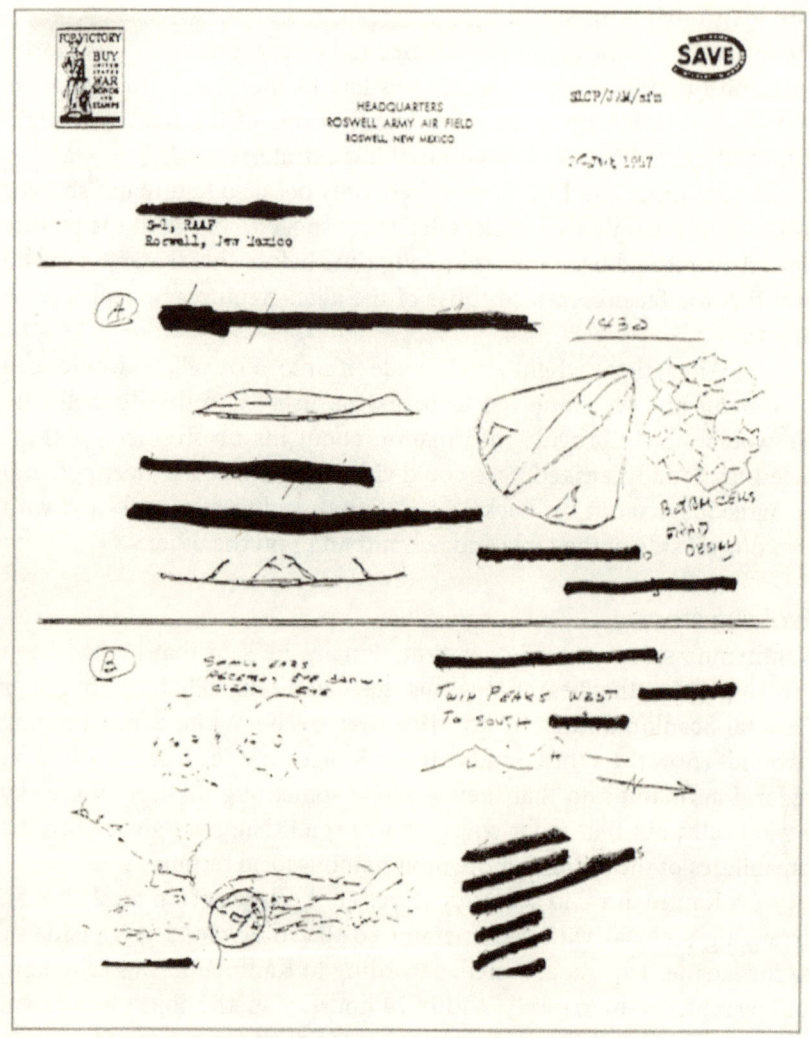

*Kaufmann's sketches of the Roswell crash.*

needs to communicate with the controlling radar and flight following center.

Or two, the craft fragmented about the time the maximum signal had been sent so that it painted each of those fragments, displaying them on the screen. It was something that had happened in the past and explains why bombers, attempting to avoid detection, sometimes drop great quantities of "chaff" – they fill the sky with tiny bits of metal, and the radar screen is filled with the blobs of light.

In any case, they knew the craft was down, they had a good idea where it went down, and they were going out to look for it. Given the radar coverage in the area and given there might not have been ground based radars in Roswell, it seems hard to believe that they would have known that it was down, or even where it might have crashed.

Kaufmann said that they drove north out of town, turned off on a side road that was little more than a scraped area across the desert, and headed to the west. There was a dull blue glow that pinpointed the location for them.

## On the scene

Once they were on the scene, in a bowl-shaped valley with some kind of strange, triangular-shaped craft impacted in the rocky cliff, they were unsure about how to proceed. The area was checked by a man with a Geiger counter and found to be relatively free of radiation; the others moved forward.

Kaufmann said that the craft was about 15 or 20 feet wide at the widest and shaped like a triangle with rounded edges. The underside had a hexagonal pattern that Kaufmann said he thought might be some kind of power cells.

Outside the craft was a body, sitting next to the cliff, looking as if it had walked over to take a nap. This creature, according to Kaufmann, was about five feet tall, had a head slightly larger than a human head, and eyes that were slightly larger than human eyes. It looked serene, as if at peace with the universe. Kaufmann said that the look on its face, and its seeming peace, always bothered him and was the one thing that stood out over all others.

Convinced there was no danger from radiation, they moved in and examined the area. Kaufmann said that Thomas was in charge, giving orders about the best ways of recovering the craft and the bodies. Kaufmann said that they cleaned the area quickly, taking the bodies to the base first, and then loading the ship onto a truck to be driven to a hangar. The craft was extremely light.

*Kaufmann at the impact site.*

According to Kaufmann, there was a core of nine men commanded by Thomas which included Kaufmann, who had the biggest responsibility for the craft and the bodies. Although Kaufmann hinted that he had been one of the more important of the nine, it would seem that his role was one of the smallest. He simply didn't have the technical expertise, authority, or education for a large role. Instead, he might have been involved simply because he was there and because Scanlon and Thomas knew him and believed they could trust him to keep the secret. Once the craft and bodies had been removed, experts in camouflage were brought in to hide the signs of the crash. When that had been completed, the military moved off, away from the scene.

## Revisiting the site

Kaufmann, nearly 50 years later, took me to where he claimed the craft had crashed. It was on a ranch now owned by Hub Corn. Back in 1947, the land had belonged to the McKnight family. Near the road that today leads to the crash site is an old, abandoned house, with little to indicate if it had stood there in 1947. Kaufmann said they had passed no house, but he seemed to think they had come into the desert farther south.

The International UFO Museum and Research Center in Roswell explored this avenue in the 1990s. They located a McKnight relative, Jim McKnight, and had him sign an affidavit about that aspect of the incident. Although he hadn't lived on the ranch in 1947, he said that he was quite familiar with the area and that all the local residents talked to one another. Had there been a UFO crash on the ranch in 1947, he was sure that he would have heard about it, but he remembered no family discussions of anything concerning UFOs.

McKnight suggested that the only place to cross the Macho River area as you headed west from the highway was near the ranch house. Anyone living there in 1947 would have seen the military as they drove in and out. Again, McKnight claimed that if anything had happened in that area, even though he was a small child in 1947 and didn't live in the area himself, he would have known about it. That he didn't suggested, to him, that nothing had happened, so that Kaufmann's story was in error.

There are, however, some subtle reasons to believe that Kaufmann might have had this inside knowledge. First, he didn't try to convince me that he had been on the debris field, an area about 75 miles northwest of Roswell, and one that was well known by the 1990s. Instead, he showed me a location closer to Roswell, but one that was hidden to the west of Highway 285. To that point, no one had suggested a site that close to the city.

## Minor corroboration

Once he had shown it to me, I began to search for corroboration. One bit of evidence came from an officer I had known for a number of years, who also claimed inside knowledge. After Kaufmann had taken me to the impact site, I asked this officer if he could show me, on a map, where he believed that the object had crashed. I provided no hint that I had seen the location as offered by Kaufmann.

That officer spent 20 minutes going over the maps, cross-checking himself. From discussions we had in the past, I believed he was going to show me a site out west of Roswell, maybe off Highway 380 as it wound its way out toward Riodoso. Instead he pointed at a location north of town within a couple of miles of what Kaufmann had shown me. The officer said, "Without a better map, that's as close as I can get."

Given that he knew nothing about what Kaufmann had told me and given that I don't believe he or Kaufmann knew one another, it was interesting that he would select, more or less, the same small section of New Mexico real estate. It was a thin corroboration of what Kaufmann had said, though it was by no means definitive.

In a similar vein, Kaufmann had told me, as he had others, that the crash took place late on the evening of July 4, 1947. Conventional wisdom suggested the crash took place on July 2, but that, according to what William Moore wrote in *The Roswell Incident*, was based on the sighting by Dan Wilmot of an object over Roswell on July 2. There certainly was no reason to connect the debris reported by Mack Brazel with the UFO seen by Wilmot.

## The guards go out

When Kaufmann made his claim that the crash took place on July 4, it did make sense out of one aspect of the case. William Woody had told me that he and his father had seen the flying saucer fall toward the ground. When they went out to search for it along Highway 285, north of Roswell, and tried to turn off to the west, they found military police guarding the roads.

Under the conventional wisdom developed by Moore and others, this meant that Woody saw the object on a Wednesday and that he and his father waited until the following Tuesday, after Brazel had been into Roswell, before they went in search of the object. Under the information supplied by Kaufmann, the object fell on a Friday and the military cordon went up on Saturday. Woody and his father would have run into the guards the next day, rather than nearly a week later. Logically, it made more sense.

There is one other, similarly subtle corroboration. One of the MPs, interviewed by me nearly 50 years after the event, said that he hadn't been directly involved in the retrieval, either as a guard or participant. He did, however, hear his fellow MPs, returning to the barracks, talk of the flying saucer. He told me that he hadn't believed them until he read about it in the newspaper.

*Hangar where alien bodies allegedly were taken.*

This means that there had been guards, cordons and retrievals prior to Brazel coming into town and prior to the publication of the information in the *Roswell Daily Record*. This corroborates the time line provided by Kaufmann and suggests that he was providing information based on his recollections rather than inventing a tale that was influenced by the publicity surrounding the Roswell case.

Kaufmann has offered some documentation to prove his involvement, though he has been tight-fisted in releasing any of it to researchers. In 1997, he showed me a letter, signed by Edwin Easley, the Roswell provost marshal in 1947, that, if verified, would end discussion about the UFO crash. Here was a document that made mention of the unusual nature of the material recovered, suggested that the bodies recovered did not appear to be human, and that the debris was unlike anything seen before or since. This document, if verified, was the smoking gun of ufology.

Kaufmann did not allow me to have a copy of it. I would have attempted to verify Easley's signature, verify the date of manufacture of the typewriter, and find other, similar documents. Although Kaufmann promised me a copy, I never received it. For researchers, the lack of copies renders the document useless. The existence of it is hearsay, and there is nothing to suggest that it is authentic.

I will note two things about that letter, however. I know precisely what it says, and I know that several others have seen it. This proves only that Kaufmann had such a letter and not that it was an authentic document signed by Easley.

## Exaggeration of his role?

And that sums up, nicely, the Kaufmann enigma. There are aspects of his story that seem to prove his veracity. There are subtle hints that he was telling the overall truth but that he might have stuck himself into the story in a role of greater importance than he had in 1947. At this point, there is no one to contradict him.

On the other hand, these little corroborations might be nothing more than coincidence. Kaufmann, having worked with General Scanlon, and unaware of his intelligence background, could have plugged him into the story because Scanlon was a real general and Kaufmann knew that he was long dead.

And, while Kaufmann might not have been overly familiar with the Roswell story when he was first identified in the early 1990s, by the middle of the decade he was well involved in it, having granted interviews to CBS and to a variety of foreign documentary makers. By 1997, he had become jaded, demanding money before he would sit down in front of a camera. Asking for compensation for an interview certainly does not invalidate the claims, but it sure raises suspicions in the minds of many.

With the Roswell case, some of the early witnesses, those that seemed to have solid tales, have fallen in recent years. Others have been challenged, but those challenges have often hinged on small, trivial discrepancies between a story told 10 or 15 years ago and one told today.

Kaufmann now skates with those with a semi-official status. He had been assigned to the Army, but as a civilian. He had been a master sergeant in the Army but promoted to a GS-11 when he was assigned to Roswell as a civilian. The GS-11 is the civilian equivalent of a company grade officer. If he knew Scanlon, and the others brought in, if he had worked with them in the past, then it is easy to believe he would have been included because they knew who he was and knew that he could be trusted.

Kaufmann's tales remain almost totally uncorroborated. If he was who he claimed, then explanations for the Roswell crash, other than the extraterrestrial, are eliminated. If he is not, then one of the best witnesses, one who claimed to have specific inside knowledge, has been eliminated. I believe Kaufmann was who he claimed, and that the Roswell crash was alien. At the moment, that makes the most sense.

*Kevin D. Randle: Well-known UFO researcher and author. With Donald R. Schmitt, he co-authored* UFO Crash at Roswell.

FATE December 2001

# The Monster and the Saucer

## Gray Barker

On September 12, 1952, the nation's wire services crackled with news of a 10-foot, redfaced monster that sprayed a foul, sickening gas and frightened seven Flatwoods, West Virginia, residents into panic.

"It looked worse than Frankenstein, Mrs. Kathleen May, one of a party who climbed a hill to investigate a flying saucer sighting, told reporters.

Shortly afterward I went to Flatwoods, a small town of 300, and spent three days subjecting these seven people, and other residents of the area, to rigorous questioning. If this story were true, I felt it deserved factual reporting; if it were a hoax I wished to explode it.

The stories I obtained from the seven different persons who had been present were heard separately. Although their accounts did not reach the terrifying proportions originally reported, and some of them had taken on color through retellings and leading questions, their stories agreed, except in very minor details. And try as I might, I could not break these stories down.

*These eyewitnesses saw a weird man-like shape on the exact spot where they are standing. Left to right: Mrs. Kathleen May, Neil Nunley, Gene Lemon, (front) Eddie May, Fred May, Ronnie Shaver and Tommy Hyer.*

On that terrifying night reports of strange lights and objects in the skies were prevalent from Ohio eastward to Washington, DC, and from Virginia northward to Pennsylvania. About seven o'clock, just as it had become dark, Mrs. May, a beautician, was told by her two small sons, Eddie, 13, and Fred, 12, that they had seen a "flying saucer" land on a hilltop above their house. The two May children had been at a nearby playground with Gene Lemon, 17, Neil Nunley, 14, Ronnie Shaver, 10, and Tommy Hyer, also 10.

The "saucer" which the children described to me "looked like a silver dollar rushing through the sky," spouting an exhaust which looked like red balls of fire. It came southwestward across the sky and, directly over the hilltop, paused, seemed to hover and descended out of view on the other side.

The group ran to Mrs. May's home, at the base of the hill, and the two May children told their mother about the object. She insisted it was "just their imaginations" until she looked upward and saw a strange red glow. Gene Lemon found a flashlight and led the party up the hill after Mrs. May agreed to accompany them.

Although not definitely timed, not more than a half-hour could have elapsed from the time of the sighting and the moment Lemon screamed with terror and fell backward, and the party fled from the sight before them.

I am now listening to tape-recorded interviews, correlating details, and sifting out those which do not exactly agree or might be colored by the horror and excitement of the moment.

The story told with least emotion is that of Neil Nunley, and the exact words I will quote will be his. Nunley impressed me as being a very level-headed and unimaginative youngster. He was very definite on what he saw and what he did not see.

He and Lemon were ahead of the others. Before them, up a roadway leading to the hilltop, they could see a reddish light pulsating from dim to bright. As they approached they encountered a mist which resembled fog, but which carried a pungent, irritating odor. It seemed to become denser as they walked farther.

As they went over the hilltop, through a gateway, they saw a globular object down over the hill to their right, about 50 feet away.

"It was just a big ball of fire," Nunley explained, and it would grow dimmer and brighter at regular intervals. He could not estimate the exact size, but others in the party said it was "big as a house."

Because their attentions were on the globe they did not notice a huge figure standing to their left, near the hilltop, until they were about 15 feet from it. Seeing two glowing green spots, which he thought were animal eyes, Lemon turned his flashlight in that direction.

Towering above them was a man-like shape. Its face was round, and blood-red. Around the face was a pointed hood-like shape, dark in appearance. In the "face" were two eye-like openings from which "greenish-orange" beams projected over their heads. The body, illuminated by the flashlight from the head downward to the waist,

*Three of the boys present at the sighting made drawings of the monster's upper portions. The drawings differ in minor details but show a basic similarity. All depict the monster's face as being round with two eye-like openings, while the head has a pointed, hood-like shape around it.*

appeared dark and colorless to Nunley, although some others said it was green. Mrs. May said she saw clothing-like folds around the figure. Descriptions from the waist down are vague; most of the seven said this part of the figure was not under view.

Not all agreed that the "monster" had arms. Mrs. May described it with terrible claws. Some said they just didn't see any. Not all agreed on the height of the figure, but according to their descriptions it couldn't have been more than 10 feet tall. It was said to have stood under an overhanging limb which is about 15 feet from the ground, and it didn't reach to this limb.

A powerful odor, described by all as sickening and irritating to the nostrils, pervaded the scene. Some had originally said it smelled like burning metal or burning sulphur, but under questioning none of the seven could remember anything in their experiences resembling the odor.

Others in the party reported a sound, coming either from the figure or the globular object, described as something between a hiss and a high-pitched squeal. They could also hear a thumping or throbbing noise.

The figure was observed for a very short while, a matter of seconds, because of the terror they experienced. It was impossible to ascertain the exact length of time it was viewed; most of the stories varied slightly. But all agreed with Nunley it was "a very short time. We just got a good look at it and left."

The figure was moving toward them but inscribing an arc, which, after viewing the scene, I estimate would lead the entity down the hillside to the globular object.

I questioned Nunley at length about the means of locomotion employed by the figure. I asked him to re-enact the scene and walk about, imitating it.

"I couldn't move as it did. It just moved. It didn't walk. It moved evenly; it didn't jump."

He could still view the figure after Lemon screamed and dropped the flashlight. The globular shape, he explained, emitted enough light to make the figure visible.

Two of the party, Mrs. May and Lemon, said they did not see the globe. They were the worst frightened, however, and their entire attention may have been centered on the figure. The Nunley boy was very definite about the globe, though; he said the reason they got so close to the monster before seeing it was because they were looking at the globe.

They had taken a dog with them, and Nunley said it howled and ran away and was found at the house with "its tail tucked between its legs."

At the house they telephoned the nearby town of Sutton, the Braxton County seat, for law officials but were told that Sheriff Robert Carr and his deputy were near Frametown, another small town about 17 miles southward, investigating the report of a plane crash. About an hour later they returned to Sutton, heard of the Flatwoods incident, and rushed to the scene. They climbed the hill, investigated, but saw, heard and smelled nothing.

I questioned A. Lee Stewart, Jr., of the *Braxton Democrat*, who arrived shortly before the sheriff and found some members of the party receiving first aid. Others were too terrified to talk coherently. He finally was able to persuade Lemon to accompany him to the hilltop.

No signs of the figure or globe were visible but bending close to the ground he could smell the strange odor, which he also described as sickening and irritating. He said while in the Air Force he had smelled gases used in warfare but had encountered nothing similar.

At seven o'clock the next morning he returned and found "skid marks" in the tall grass, leading from the spot where the figure was seen to where the globe was reported. The earth was not disturbed, but small stones had been tossed aside.

I have been over the site carefully. I saw marks and a huge area of grass trampled down, but multitudes have visited and walked over the location. I believe Stewart's observations are accurate, however. I could see no trace of the oil reported to have been present on the ground and to have saturated the weeds with an odd, gummy deposit; but there had been a rain. Some said samples of the deposit were being analyzed but I could not track down the information.

Although Flatwoods residents shake their heads and discredit the story, attributing the phenomenon to anything from a buck deer with white breast to the dome of the State House, allegedly stolen and flown to Washington by the party in power, there have arisen dozens of variations, each more hair-raising than the one before.

I ran down a number of rumors. I drove 50 miles to interview a man who had claimed to be present when a space ship had taken off from the hill. He told me he had not seen this occur but had been present shortly after the incident and seen an object in the air. It was round, with a flat top, orange in color. Streams of fire, like jets, were projecting downward. He agreed to meet me that evening, drive to Flatwoods with me and point out the exact spot over which the object had circled and then flown southwestward. He did not keep the appointment.

Numerous people in a 20-mile radius saw illuminated objects in the sky at the same time. I could have spent a month interviewing all such viewers. The objects were described mainly as round, red or orange in color and spouting fire.

These objects were reported flying in various directions, although the progress of some of them could be charted. It is evident that either they saw different objects, or one object was making a circuit of the area.

Mayor J. Holt Byrne of Sutton, also editor of his *Braxton Central,* put the inevitable question to me.

"Well, what do you think it was?"

Sitting in his newspaper office, surrounded by the hustle and bustle of a busy small town, I should have liked to say, "The misinterpretation of natural phenomena." In my belief, I told him, the account fits perfectly with others of flying saucers or similar craft.

I believe that such a vehicle landed on the hillside, either from necessity or to make observations.

The monster could have been a robot from the globular ship, or some entity inside a suit which would adapt the wearer to Earth's atmosphere. When the flashlight was shone upon it, that stimulus then would start the creature on its way back to the ship. Or perhaps it did not see or take notice of the seven odd bipeds that had come to view it and, had they waited, might have completed its progress to the ship and left.

But that is speculation. What I do know is that when you talk to seven people with honesty and fear in their eyes you know in your heart when they are telling the truth. These people did see something. And whatever they saw was very much like what they described.

*Gray Barker (1925-84): Ufologist, writer, author and sometimes hoaxer. Barker introduced the concept of Men In Black into UFO folklore in his book* They Knew Too Much About Flying Saucers. *He lived in West Virginia.*

FATE January 1953

# Inside the Flying Saucers... Pancakes
## Paul Foght

"The hatch opened underneath and a man in a black suit got out. He had this water jug and he gestured to me to give him some water, so I did."

That's how Joe Simonton describes his now famous contact with the flying saucer he says landed in his backyard at Eagle River, Wisconsin on April 18, 1961.

If this saucer was the same vehicle that was subsequently reported four additional times in Joe's neighborhood, from April 18 to 27, it is no wonder the crew needed a drink. They were a pretty busy crowd.

Each of these Wisconsin saucer stories involves witnesses of apparently unimpeachable character and integrity. The report of Joe Simonton's status in his community, and his detailed and voluntary reports to three separate legal authorities in his community, were strong factors in influencing the Air Force to order complete and immediate investigation of his claims.

Joe Simonton, the plumber-farmer-auctioneer from Eagle River, now has had his history, habits and complexes probed and sifted by Air

Force investigators, newspaper men and television commentators. Out of all this come these conclusions:

For the Air Force, Dr. J. Allen Hynek, consultant, Aerospace Technical Intelligence Center, reports that Joe Simonton has "all his marbles" and is telling a straightforward story. Dr. Hynek believes there is "no question that Mr. Simonton felt that his contact had been a real experience." The Air Force is now conducting a chemical study of a cake given Joe by the saucer crew.

From the National Investigations Committee for Aerial Phenomena (NICAP), Richard Hall reports the committee is "highly skeptical" of Joe's story. The committee might analyze one of Joe's cakes which was sent to it by an Eagle River judge [who had been given the cake by Simonton] and will probably conduct a "routine investigation."

Joe Simonton reports in person, "I don't care what anybody else believes, I just know what I saw. If it happened again, I don't think I'd tell anybody about it."

The fact is Joe almost did keep his story a secret at the very beginning. He says that the saucer landed at 11 AM on Tuesday, April 18, but Joe apparently first revealed his story two days later to Vilas County Judge Frank Carter, who has been long interested in flying saucer reports. Joe then made further reports to District Attorney Calvin Burton and to Sheriff John Schroeder. Here is his story as he told it:

"Before I saw it, I heard this terrible swirling noise above my house. At first, I thought the whole house was going to blow away. Then I walked over to the window and saw this saucer come straight down, vertically. I run out real quick. Then the hatch opened underneath and a man in a black suit, nearly five feet tall, got out. I never saw anything like it.

"He had this water jug and he gestured to me to give him some water, so I did. When I went over I got a look inside and saw the other men. They didn't say anything to me. I pointed to the pancakes by the instrument panel and they gave me a few.

"Then the first man got inside and the saucer took off again at a 45-degree angle, with such a whoosh that nearby pine trees were bowed over."

Joe Simonton described the saucer as a gleaming silver, brighter-than-chrome machine that appeared to hover over the ground instead of landing. He estimated that it was about 12 feet from top to bottom and

*Joe Simonton with one of the alien pancakes.*

about 30 feet in diameter. He recalls that he noted exhaust pipes six or seven inches in diameter along the edge of the saucer.

The interior of the ship was black, almost the color of wrought iron, Simonton said. From the interior of the craft came a slow, whining sound like the hum of a generator. The hatch through which he peered into the ship was about five feet off the ground. When the craft lifted off, Simonton said the large hatch snapped shut and was machined so smoothly he could scarcely detect where the hatch was after it closed.

When the ship took off it went up slowly to a height of about 15 feet. But then, Simonton reported, "in two seconds it was so far away I couldn't see it." The ship moved off in a southerly direction as it left, he said.

Simonton saw three men in the machine, all dressed in black two-piece suits. He judged that they were about five feet tall and weighed about 125 pounds. He said they were smooth-shaven and resembled men of Latin descent.

None of the "saucernauts" in the ship spoke with Simonton, but they did give him souvenirs [the pancakes] which are the only physical evidence of their contact with Joe.

Joe collected his souvenirs when he noticed that "one of the men in the ship was frying food on a flameless grill of some sort." He motioned to indicate an interest in their food, and one of the men, also dressed in black but with a narrow red trim along the trousers, handed him three small cakes.

A portion of one of these cakes was given to the Air Force investigating team and is now being analyzed by their chemists. An entire cake was sent to the National Investigations Committee for Aerial Phenomena, but that group's arrangements for an analysis broke down and the cake is now reported to be growing a luxuriant mold in a Washington, DC refrigerator.

These cakes are the only evidence of the "saucernauts" visit with Joe Simonton. After Joe reported the visit to his local sheriff, two deputies were sent to the scene to search for physical evidence, but they found nothing out of place in the farmyard.

There is no radar evidence of the flight and no photos of the ship. Air Force Investigator Dr. Hynek, who is also chairman of the astronomy department at Northwestern University, reported that the space vehicle was not detected by the Air Force radar center at Truax Field, Madison, Wisconsin. Of course, Air Force radar couldn't find the hijacked Portuguese cruise ship, the 20,000-ton *Santa Maria*, either.

Dr. Hynek was disappointed that Mr. Simonton was not able to take a photo of his visitors and their ship. In addition, Dr. Hynek reports that in his 12 years of investigating UFOs and flying saucer contacts for the Air Force, he never has located a photo that could be identified beyond any doubt as a flying machine or mass of unknown origin.

The Air Force feels that Joe Simonton's Eagle River visitors present a good example of a saucer contact case, and consequently a complete investigation was begun even though the Air Force normally does not conduct extensive inquiries of reported sightings or contacts where only one witness is involved. Joe Simonton's story was investigated by Dr. Hynek and Major Robert Friend, both representing the Aerospace Technical Intelligence Center, and by an officer from the K. I. Sawyer Air Force Base, Gwinn, Michigan.

Among the circumstances that indicated the advisability of a complete investigation of Mr. Simonton's story were reports from the scene that Joe is a sober and sensible person.

Joe has lived in the Eagle River community for 30 years, serves as the Chamber of Commerce's Santa Claus each Christmas, and enjoys an excellent reputation with local authorities. Sheriff John Schroeder reported, "Joe really believes everything he says, and he isn't a drinking man. He talks sensibly."

County Judge Frank Carter says he is convinced Simonton actually saw the "saucernauts" because he is unable to think of any way in which Simonton could profit if the story were a hoax.

The judge's part in the Eagle River case has attracted some attention because he also is known as an entertainer, serving at church and club functions as a magician, ventriloquist and hypnotist. However, investigation has not established any unusual connection between the saucer fan judge and Joe Simonton.

The Air Force investigators have indicated that they realize Mr. Simonton will be subjected to ridicule from some sources for his story, but the Air Force hopes that qualified and competent witnesses will not be discouraged from making reports of saucer sightings. The clearing house for such information is the Aerospace Technical Intelligence Center, Wright Patterson Air Force Base, Dayton, Ohio.

Joe Simonton's story of his contact with the saucer immediately produced four other reports of sightings in the Eagle River area. Savino Borgo, an Eagle River insurance agent, said he had seen a saucer while driving on Wisconsin Highway 70 about a mile from Simonton's home at about the same time Simonton said the saucer landed in his yard.

Two other men, Gibb Sanborn, manager of the Wisconsin State Employment Service office at Eagle River, and Jack Long, a Boulder Junction, Wisconsin merchant, said they also had sighted saucers recently.

A report which has interested the Air Force investigators came in on April 27 from Rhinelander, Wisconsin, about 20 miles from Eagle River. Air Force interest was apparently triggered by the report of five witnesses to this sighting.

At 6:45 PM on April 27, 1961 Brent Lorbetski, 20, and Tim Hunt, 17, were in an automobile near the Lorbetski home in Sugar Camp Township near the city of Rhinelander.

The young men spotted a high flying, silver-colored circular object. The object was passing overhead at considerable altitude and at high speed but was making no noise.

The youths called to the other members of Lorbetski's family who came outside in time to see the object. The family then reported the sighting to the Oneida County Sheriff's office. Brent Lorbetski's father, who was not home at the time of the sighting, is chairman of the town of Sugar Camp. Inquiries to local authorities indicate that all the witnesses have excellent reputations for reliability and veracity.

FATE's inquiry into the Rhinelander sighting has revealed that some skeptics in Rhinelander feel that the local sighting was authentic but that the sightings in nearby Eagle River probably have something to do with stimulating the tourist trade.

Until the Air Force completes and announces the results of its chemical analysis of the "saucernaut" cake given to them by Mr. Simonton, this latest series of sightings will have added nothing concrete to the body of information on flying saucers. Unless, however, it is this observation: if a flying saucer lands in your town, that's reality; if you hear one has appeared in a neighboring town, that's a hoax.

*[Editor's note: Simonton ate part of one of the pancakes and said it tasted like cardboard. A test of one pancake revealed it to be of terrestrial origin, according to the Food and Drug Laboratory of the US Department of Health, Education, and Welfare. The identified ingredients were hydrogenated fat, starch, buckwheat hulls, soybean hulls and wheat bran. Perhaps the aliens were experimenting with human food?]*

FATE August 1961

# UFOs, Mothman and Me

## John A. Keel

I was pushed into the flying saucer fracas in 1966 by a *Playboy* editor who wanted a "definitive" article on the subject. The first logical step was to seek out experts. I quickly discovered there weren't any. There were people who called themselves experts, all wallowing in egocentric delusions of self-importance, all feuding with their fellow experts. Paranoia was rampant in the field and every teenager and little old lady in tennis shoes involved in UFO hunting was convinced the government, and particularly the Air Force and CIA, was spending millions to mess up their personal mail and telephones. There was a big overlap, too, of wild-eyed right-wingers, and many of the more bizarre beliefs of the John Birch Society and even the KKK were absorbed into the UFO lore.

### Air Force lies

A few UFO books, mostly in the crackpot category, had been published in the 1950s, but copies of them were now almost impossible to locate. (The average UFO book sells about 3,000 copies, even today – a pathetically small number when you consider how much publicity UFOs have received.) Ivan Sanderson, zoologist, author and well-known TV personality, had a library of some of the better books. He lived on a farm in the wilds of northern New Jersey. A charismatic Briton usually surrounded by hordes of visitors, Ivan had single-handedly introduced the subject of the Abominable Snowman and Bigfoot to the American public. We met originally because I had once tracked the elusive Abominable Snowman in the Himalayas and Ivan was preparing to write a massive book on those hairy horrors. He was also a longtime observer of the UFO scene and at the beginning of my quest he gave me the best advice I would receive. "Don't take this flying saucer business too seriously," he warned me. "Just think of the whole thing as an intellectual exercise."

I made several trips to Washington and the Pentagon in an earnest effort to present the Air Force's side of the controversy fairly. The various Air Force officials openly and repeatedly lied to me about several things. Their biggest fears were that the public would discover that they didn't know a thing about flying saucers and that the scope of the phenomenon was much broader than any casual observer might think. UFOs were, and are, successfully eluding our defensive systems and landing frequently in farm fields, on highways and even – believe it or not – on airport runways. They have been causing considerable damage to property for many years.

A Pentagon officer once told me that it cost $10,000 to investigate a single UFO sighting. I tried for a long time to get the Project Bluebook budget, but it was buried in the general public-relations budget and couldn't be extricated. According to a secretary, their biggest task was answering "kiddie mail." However, one day when I was visiting Lieutenant Colonel Maston Jacks, a girl came into the office and put a newspaper clipping into a big red folder marked Top Secret, so maybe a clipping service was part of their expenses.

My brushes with civilian experts, Air Force apologists and scientists convinced me there was only one way to find out what was going on. I would have to go into the field and investigate some fresh sightings first-hand.

## Enter the Mothman

In November 1966 four young people in Point Pleasant, West Virginia, reported a chilling encounter with a seven-foot-tall monster with glowing red eyes and a 10-foot wingspan. The press labeled it Mothman, and during the next year more than 100 West Virginians would see it. If it had been just another 10-foot-tall hairy monster I would have ignored the report. After all, Bigfoot sightings were superabundant. But the West Virginia critter had wings, could take off straight up like a helicopter and was fond of pursuing automobiles at 90 miles an hour. In short, he was my kind of weirdie.

I found Point Pleasant was a quiet little town of 6,300 people, dozens of churches and no public bars. The Mothman sightings had taken place in a desolate World War II ammunition dump on the edge of town. More intriguing, there had been countless UFO sightings up and

*Mothman.*

down the Ohio River all year. Eerie diamond-brilliant lights passed over Point Pleasant every night at 8:30 on a regular schedule. I decided to do something that the Air Force and the loud-mouthed UFO buffs had never thought of doing. I decided to investigate the situation instead of just holding conversations with the witnesses.

Within a few days a much bigger picture began to evolve. The region was not only haunted by strange aerial lights, but the homes of the witnesses were plagued with poltergeists and other supernatural phenomena. Television sets were burning out at an alarming rate. Telephones were going crazy, ringing at all hours of the day and night with no one on the other end. Some people were getting calls from mysterious strangers speaking a cryptic language. Black Cadillacs bearing Oriental-looking gentlemen were cruising the black hills of West Virginia.

Mothman assumed minor importance as I uncovered all these other things. I had been investigating psychic manifestations all over the world for years and I recognized the pattern here. Some UFOs were directly related to the human consciousness, just as ghostly apparitions are often the product of the percipient's mind. There are deeply rooted psychic and psychological factors in the UFO phenomenon, and the sudden appearance of a light in the sky triggers and releases the human energy that stimulated seemingly supernatural events. We cannot define the exact nature of those lights, but we can catalog the many manifestations that accompany them, and we can demonstrate how identical manifestations occur in many different frames of reference. Religious apparitions are kissin' kin with the tall, stately Michael Rennie types that claim to come from Ganymede, Uranus, Clarion (an unknown planet on the other side of the sun) and a dozen other absurd places. The "miracle" at Fatima, Portugal, in 1917 was undoubtedly the best-documented UFO sighting of all time (70,000 witnesses) and certainly the most thoroughly investigated.

## Men In Black

Unfortunately, those interested in flying saucers had no interest at all in psychic phenomena, and vice versa. Those who were busy trying to trap a Bigfoot frowned upon all other forms of the weird and supernatural. Yet sea serpents, Abominable Snowpersons, poltergeists, frog rainfalls, and UFOs are all interrelated. You can't possibly investigate one without some knowledge of the others. For example, the Men In Black (MIBs) so well known in UFO lore are even better known in the histories of witchcraft and black magic. These mysterious gentlemen have been reported for a thousand years. The UFO buffs decided they were CIA agents. But another group known as superbuffs thinks the whole world is run by a secret league of wealthy men and that the MIBs are their minions. In the Far East, where belief in a "king of the world" still rides high, people think the MIBs are agents from the secret underground cities of the king. In West Virginia the MIBs passed themselves off as everything from Bible salesmen to census takers.

When I returned to New York City from that first trip to West Virginia my own telephone went berserk. At first I had problems only when I was speaking to Ivan Sanderson in New Jersey. He was on one of those freak pseudo-independent phone company lines and it was common to be drowned out by static, or have the call suddenly cut off. Ivan solved the problem by shouting obscenities into the phone. Strangely, it worked. It was not uncommon to be having a conversation with this dignified Briton when clicks and other noises would cause him to pause and then bellow, "Get off this line, you god-damned son of a bitch!" The line noises would cease abruptly.

My problems soon escalated. Someone would interrupt my conversations with a sound like a one-stringed guitar. The sound of an extension being picked up could be clearly heard. The telephone company ignored my complaints, naturally, until I wrote directly to the president of the company. Then fur flew. They checked out my line and happily reported that I did not have one tap on my wire – I had two! I demanded that they find out who was tapping my phone, but they said they couldn't do that.

## Moronic harassments

I lived in a large apartment building and there was a telephone room in the basement where thousands of wires converged and connected to underground cables. Somehow someone managed to get into this locked room, search out my wires from all the thousands of others and cut them with a pair of pliers. This someone accomplished this not once, but twice. I went with the repairman when they checked my line and the second time I demanded that the whole matter be put in writing. So, someone in the main office sent me a letter stating my phone had been out of order because a piece of solder had come loose in the main installation!

Ma Bell wasn't the only member of the flying-saucer conspiracy. My mailman was in on it, too. Suddenly my letters were going astray or were being mysteriously opened. Just so I would know my mail was being monitored, someone would Xerox letters sent to me, keep the originals and reseal the Xerox copies in the envelopes. Even letters from my mother were Xeroxed!

Now I began to understand why so many UFO buffs were paranoid. Obviously, a great deal of money, time and personnel went into these moronic harassments. A friend of mine who once served in Army Intelligence tells how his unit was kept busy tailing and harassing completely innocent victims. I suspect that some worthless bureaucratic boondoggle was assigned the UFO beat, not out of maliciousness but just to give them something to do. I eventually discovered that another phone was hooked up to my line and had been getting my calls while I was getting their bills – as much as $400 a month. And my mail was going first to another address before it was passed on to me. What stunned me was that the other address was a building housing Ma Bell's long-distance equipment! Proof positive that the telephone company was plotting to take over the world.

Meanwhile, back in West Virginia, Mothman was continuing to chase automobiles. I returned to Point Pleasant several times in 1967, learning more about the phenomenon with each trip. Several contactees (people who thought they had met the flying saucer occupants) had emerged and I was hypnotizing them and studying them carefully. I found these people had two levels of memory. The first level, the surface level, recalled under hypnosis a fascinating adventure, usually of being taken aboard a wonderful flying saucer. But the hidden level, which was difficult to get at and usually took several hypnotic sessions before it could be reached, rejected the false memory (confabulation) and painted a different picture. Most of these contactees had been transported to a van or house where they were subjected to brain-washing techniques and injected with an unknown substance. Then they were given a confabulation to remember and were released.

But no matter how hard I tried I couldn't find out who was doing this. The whole contactee syndrome was a fraud, but the contactees were innocent victims. Why was anyone going to all the trouble to create these contactees? Many people in West Virginia told me of seeing strange, unmarked vans cruising the back roads at night.

Another thing that bothered me was the widespread slaughter of domestic animals during the UFO waves. The animals, usually cows, sheep and dogs, had all the blood drained from their bodies and their sex organs removed with surgical precision. I saw one cow cut in half as cleanly as if it had been done with a giant pair of scissors. These animal mutilations were at first confined to the Northeast in the 1960s, but in the 1970s they spread to the Midwest.

## Simpleminded games

I spent many miserable days wading around farm fields in West Virginia to inspect mutilated animals, and many cold and scary nights on hilltops watching funny lights cavort in the sky. When I signaled them with a flashlight in Morse code they actually responded. If I flashed the word "descend," they would drop downward in the falling-leaf motion made famous in so many reports.

*John A. Keel with Mothman figurine.*

Were they spaceships from another world? Not very likely. They seemed like mischievous masses of energy playing simpleminded games with a simpleminded human. As a professional simpleton I have seen so many of these strange lights that I have lost count. The sheer quantity of these objects and the frequency of their appearances negates the extraterrestrial hypothesis (ETH). During UFO waves they appear in a thousand places around the world simultaneously on a single date. Would a society on some other planet send thousands of craft to this world to hover around garbage dumps, stone quarries, golf courses and cemeteries (all favorite UFO haunts) for one night, or one week and then fly home across millions of miles in space?

These things have been around for thousands of years and they have been seen in the same places century after century. They are part of the environment, like clouds and pollution.

Mothman, like phantom kangaroos and the redoubtable Bigfoot, belongs to that class of beasties known to the ancient Greeks as Chimeras.

The Greeks noted that such animals usually had fiery red eyes, were often surrounded by the smell of "fire and brimstone" (hydrogen sulfide) and often disappeared as suddenly and mysteriously as they had come.

In countless UFO cases we also find all of these characteristics. The UFO is surrounded by a terrible smell, like the smell of rotten eggs (hydrogen sulfide again), sometimes making the witnesses ill. Creatures emerge from the UFO and leave footprints leading to the middle of a muddy field, where they vanish suddenly. Or they leave no footprints at all.

Chimeras take many forms. A few years back there were reliable reports of dinosaurs stomping around Italy, France, Africa and even Texas. Some of them left perfect dinosaur tracks behind. Mothman left tracks that looked like giant dog prints. Such prints have been found in many places where other types of monsters have been seen. Even gigantic snakes – and we have plenty of reports of those—have left giant dog prints in their wake.

## Cosmic jokers

When you investigate a UFO flap area very carefully the whole phenomenon begins to seem like a robust practical joke perpetrated by some cosmic jokers. There is no beginning and no end. What happened in West Virginia in 1966 was repeated in Texas in 1976 when a giant bird, identified as a prehistoric pterodactyl by some witnesses, put in a brief appearance.

We know now that many of the things that happen in UFO country are clever diversions. While armed citizenry go chasing after UFOs in one direction, animals in a field in the opposite direction are suddenly mutilated. Mothman kept a whole town sitting in an old ammunition dump for several weeks while animal mutilations and human abductions took place only a few miles away.

In earlier times, the manifestations were blamed on black magic practitioners, witches, alchemists, the Fairy Commonwealth, the Rosicrucians, the Gypsies. Now we know that whoever is behind it all has the ability to use advanced techniques of hypnosis and brainwashing. Dr. Leon Davidson, one of the men who gave us the atomic bomb (thank you, doctor), studied the UFO situation for years and finally decided it was all a cold war gambit of the CIA. When UFO mania struck Tashkent in the Soviet Union back in the 1960s, the Russian news agency, Tass, issued a release accusing the Western imperialists of being behind the whole thing. Ivan Sanderson stuck his tongue in his cheek and wrote a book explaining that UFOs were coming from cities at the bottom of our oceans. Ray Palmer, the man who started it all when he was editor of *Amazing Stories* back in the 1940s, believed that the earth was hollow and that UFOs were coming to us from holes in the North and South Poles.

The situation is infinitely more complex than any of these interesting but simplistic explanations. If UFOs are real, and if they are extraterrestrial, then all the patterns indicate they are totally hostile. If this is the case, then the proper government procedure would be to set up a false PR front to deal with the random reports and lull the public while a secret agency made a real effort to cope with the problem. If they are not real but are only part of the wild, wild world of psychic phenomena and Chimeras, then there is nothing that can be done and no amount of investigating can be expected to be fruitful. So, it is a no-win dilemma for the civilian saucer sleuth with a straitjacket as the reward.

I wish I could report that the Mothman episode had a happy ending and that the people of Point Pleasant returned to normal, industrious lives. Unfortunately, 13 months to the day after the creature's first appearance a terrible disaster struck the little town. The bridge that joined Point Pleasant with Ohio collapsed laden with rush-hour traffic and 46 people died. Several of them had seen Mothman and/or UFOs. The critter appeared a couple of times following the bridge disaster, then vanished forever.

*John A. Keel (1930-2009): A longtime student and author of Fortean phenomena and other mysteries of existence; prolific journalist, writer and author; FATE columnist. His book* The Mothman Prophecies *was made into a film released in 2002.*

FATE September 2007
Excerpted from a publication of The New York Fortean Society, 1980, 1991.

# Russian Submarines and Unidentified Submersible Objects

## Paul Stonehill

V.V. Krapiva, a researcher and writer who resides in Odessa, Ukraine, years ago had attended numerous lectures presented by veteran officers of Soviet nuclear-powered submarines. They had served in the Soviet North, aboard secret naval installations and bases. The lectures sometimes veered off from the planned presentations, and many spellbinding tales were told as a result. For instance, episodes when Soviet sonar operators (military hydro-acoustics technicians) were hearing strange targets present at great depths. Soviet Navy submarines were being chased by other submarines.

**Mysterious object pursues**

The pursuers changed their speed at will; speeds that were much greater than any other similar vessel in the world could produce at that time. Lieutenant Commander Oleg Sokolov confidentially informed the students that while on duty during his submarine's navigation, he had observed through a periscope an ascent of some strange object in the water. He was not able to identify it, because he viewed it through the optical system of the periscope. This underwater takeoff took place in the early 1960s.

An interesting observation of a UFO was recorded by a crew of a Soviet nuclear submarine in 1965. This case is on file in the Colonel Kolchin archives. All those who had observed the UFO were ordered to report the details and provide drawings to the Special Department (i.e., Naval Intelligence). The submarine was to rendezvous with a ship in the Atlantic Ocean. They arrived at the meeting place an hour-and-a-half before the time of the rendezvous, and the captain allowed the crew to come to the outside deck. No ships were in the area, and the sky was starry and cloudless. Then the watchman observed a cigar-shaped object moving noiselessly through the sky. Although the submarine was in international waters at the time, the Soviets assumed the unidentified object was American, and decided to dive immediately. But their onboard radar did not record anything, and the captain decided to stay put, above water. Suddenly three rays shot out from the UFO, and the Soviet submariners noticed something very unusual about the object.

The UFO had no gondolas, and no horizontal or vertical rudders. The object was about 200-250 meters long, and Soviet submariners were not familiar with such dirigibles, for those used by American Air Force were much smaller. Then something strange took place: the UFO slowly descended to the surface of the ocean, its searchlights still on, about half a mile from the submarine, and dived underwater. The submarine's sonar had registered a strange and very intensive hissing sound, as the UFO submerged, but the sound was of a very short duration.

## Reports from Kuzovkin

A well-known Soviet UFO researcher and author, A. S. Kuzovkin, had been engaged in UFO research ever since he observed one such object in 1964. He was a physicist and researched the ecology of anomalous phenomena for *Vokrug Sveta*, a very popular Soviet magazine. Kuzovkin mentioned in his writings that while visiting Sevastopol, a port city in Ukraine, he met with local marine scientists who had descended into the depths of the Black Sea in deep water bathyscaphes. They observed,

*Russian submarine.*

among other things, an object that resembled a wheel as large as a 10-story building, standing vertically underwater. The scientists saw and later described to Kuzovkin the "wheel" that would remain immobile for a while, and then move into a horizontal position, rotate and depart.

Another well-known Russian researcher of the paranormal and author, Aleksandr Petukhov, mentioned an incident from 1951. It took place in the territorial waters of the USSR. A Soviet submarine encountered a strange underwater object of gigantic size; it did not react to the submarine communication to identify itself and continued an unhurried movement toward the nation's shores. The captain of the submarine ordered depth bombs to be dropped into the site where USO was located. The unidentified object did not react to the attack, and continued its course, at the same speed. After a while it unexpectedly and abruptly ascended to the surface of the sea. At the depth of 50 meters it stopped its ascent, changed the course, and departed.

### *Yargora* sighting

In July of 1978, there was a UFO sighting in the Mediterranean. The captain of the Soviet motor ship *Yargora* immediately sent a radiogram about it to the Soviet Academy of Sciences. The coordinates of the sighting were 37 degrees northern latitude and 3 degrees 40 minutes of eastern longitude. The time was between 7:30 and 8:40 in the morning. The object that was observed by Soviet seamen was shaped like a flattened-out sphere, its color that of a white pearl. There were three protruding constructions in the bottom portion of the UFO; they resembled antennae. The object moved from east to westward direction.

No reply to the radiogram ever came from the Academy. This sighting was mentioned in the 2001 article written by Valentin Psalomschikov and published in *NLO* magazine. An unnamed Russian source mentioned that *Yargora's* Captain Cherepanov sent a telegram from the ship to Moscow, Soviet Academy of Sciences, regarding the sighting.

On December 26, 2002, the Russian newspaper *Zhizn* published an article about Soviet observations of UFOs. The chairman of the Anomalous Phenomena Commission of the Russian Geographical Society in Saint Petersburg made a presentation at the society's monthly meeting. The society, founded in 1980, had studied tens of thousands of cases of UFO sightings, and had reached the conclusion that UFOs are real.

The chairman at the time, Yevgeny Litvinov, recalled that his experience with the UFOs had begun when he was a Soviet Navy officer and did not take seriously any published UFO-related information. Then came the winter of 1979-80, and several incidents had rocked the Northern Fleet, forcing the Soviet general staff to take UFOs seriously. UFOs had visited a Soviet submarine base at the Western Dvina [river] every week during a six-month period.

The craft were shaped like disks, and hovered over the armaments (mines, torpedoes and nuclear weapons) preparation sites. The UFOs also flew above the top secret Soviet military town. While the military personnel below freely observed the "flying saucers," the anti-aircraft radars did not register anything. Captain Beregovoy, head of the Naval Intelligence for the Northern Fleet, ordered that photographs of the UFOs be taken, but to no avail; the film turned out to be accidentally exposed each time.

The Soviets were busy trying to find out the nature of UFOs flying over their heads. Initially they suspected NATO, but then it was explained to them that potential adversaries do not possess such technology. To prevent panic, those in command told their military personnel that the UFOs above were Soviet-made craft, and that tests were underway. Of course, high-ranking officers knew better, and felt terrified by the uncertainty.

Rather serious incidents took place during that winter. The crew of a Soviet Project 671 submarine ("Victor" class sub, per NATO classification) encountered a UFO. The sub's commander was Aleksey Korzhev. The sub was coming to the base; sometimes it surfaced, sometimes it would descend to 200 meters. They wanted to be undetected by spy satellites. Then they received a report that up and straight ahead was an airplane. The commander was surprised, for the weather was absolutely not conducive for aircraft flights. But 50 meters from the sub a silvery disc was hovering, slowly moving with the sub, staying a bit ahead of it. The crew looked at it, feeling mesmerized. Then the UFO emitted a ray of light, and this pillar of bright white light did not immediately reach the surface of the water, but contrary to the laws of physics, it slowly descended. Korzhev immediately ordered a change of the ship's course. The disc slowly ascended and disappeared in the clouds. Litvinov said that the Soviets speculated that the UFO wanted to scan the submarine that happened to carry new weapons aboard.

## Soroka's report

Mikhail Soroka, a paranormal phenomena researcher from Kiyiv, Ukraine, also described the same incident in more detail in an interview he gave to *FAKTY* newspaper (December 2007). Soroka mentioned fascinating details of the USO encounter when a nuclear submarine was accompanying a surface vessel. The submarine surfaced, and a large object appeared in the sky. Its shape was that of a mushroom with its cap turned down. Its bottom part shone white light; the part above shone yellow light; the next part shone reddish light; and the uppermost part shone bright red light. The object not only approached the ships but also directed toward one of them a ray from its searchlight. Then the object unexpectedly disappeared. He also mentioned that Soviet Navy's intelligence believed that UFOs generally appeared over military vessels and coastal installations.

Later, when Litvinov was with the special commission of the Soviet Navy's main staff, he was able to read dozens of UFO reports that came from the intelligence channels. One report described a UFO landing in Motovsky Bay in the Barents Sea. Years later, a leakage of liquid radioactive waste from a spent fuel storage facility took place in the Motovsky Bay and Litsa Fjord.

Zapadnaya Litsa is the largest and most important Russian naval base for nuclear-powered submarines. The base is located on the Litsa Fjord at the westernmost point of the Kola Peninsula, about 45 kilometers from the Norwegian border. The Litsa Fjord heads into the Kola Peninsula interior from the Motovsky Fjord, just across from the southeastern coast of the Rybachky Peninsula.

Few people in the West know exactly what was going on there during the Soviet rule. No radar station in the vicinity registered the UFOs. Soviet experts assumed that an ionized cloud enveloped the UFOs.

Another incident, mentioned by Litvinov to *Zhizn*, comes from the archives of the Russia's Geographic Society. It took place in the Mediterranean in November 1976. Soviet diesel submarine Project 641 ("Foxtrot" per NATO classification), navigated through the Gibraltar, and surfaced. It was 2 AM, and the sea was absolutely still. The captain, the watch officer and signalman came to the submarine deck to verify the vessel's coordinates.

Suddenly they noticed a radiant silvery sphere to the left, over the horizon. The sphere ascended rapidly, and suddenly they saw right in front of the sub, on the water, a radiant map of the Mediterranean. It appeared at precisely the moment when the navigator was to determine the sub's location measuring the position of stars. The impression was that someone aboard the sphere read the Russia navigator's thoughts. Moreover, the radiant map also indicated the sub's position. The sphere flew away, and the map disappeared.

## Causes investigated

Yevgeny Litvinov revealed in the interview that he is convinced that UFOs exist, but he puts aside his convictions when he is asked to determine the veracity of reports. He has developed a complex method for systematic selection (as is done by intelligence officers). His scale of credible authenticity is based on 350 criteria.

Litvinov has concluded that out of all data, about 70 percent result from technogenic reasons, natural phenomena or mystification. But the other 30 percent are real observations of UFOs. There are too many of them to simply wave them away. His database contains 10,000 observations and incidents. Litvinov stated that most often UFOs are observed over military installations, areas of ecological disasters and geological faults.

In the 1970s, reports issued by Admiral V. A. Domislovsky, chief of the Pacific Fleet's intelligence department, described an unknown, gigantic cylindrical object sighted by Soviet Navy in faraway regions of the Pacific Ocean. The object was 800-900 meters long. When it hovered over the ocean, smaller objects exited from one of its ends (like bees from a beehive) and descended into the waters. Sometime later they reentered the gigantic UFO. After the smaller objects entered, the UFO would fly away and disappear over the horizon. This information was revealed in Vladimir Ajaja's interviews to Russian media.

## Too fast for comfort

According to MosNews.com (July 16, 2009), former Rear Admiral and nuclear submarine commander Yury Beketov was quoted describing events that occurred in the Bermuda Triangle. "We repeatedly observed that the instruments detected the movements of material objects at unimaginable speed, around 230 knots (400 km per hour [250 mph]). It's hard to reach that speed on the surface – only in the air [is it readily possible]… The beings that created those material objects significantly exceed us in development."

Russian Naval intelligence expert and Captain First Rank Igor Barklay noted that the unidentified objects were most often spotted in deep water near where military forces are concentrated off the Bahamas, Bermuda, Puerto Rico and the east coast of the United States.

The February issue of the remarkable Belarus newspaper *Sekretnie Issledovaniya* (Issue 3{212}), contained an article written by Valeriya Peresilkina. Titled *"Zagadki glubin"* ("Secrets of the depths"), it lists cases of USOs observed by the Russian Navy in various seas of our planet.

The author mentions Captain First Rank (retired) Yuri Vinogradov who had served in the Soviet Navy from 1975 to 2000. A top expert in his field, he had been involved in a number of submarine search and recovery operations. He was a veteran of high-risk units, and a participant in four long-range missions. He had been to the Devil's Sea, also known as the Dragon Triangle. It is located between Japan, Guam, and northern Philippines. Some call this area the Pacific Bermuda Triangle.

In the 1980s, Vinogradov had participated in the search and rescue operations of the Soviet Pacific Fleet (submarines and surface vessels had been involved). Twice he and other officers had observed, on the sonar screen, a USO that moved at great speed, and disappeared in the depths.

*Paul Stonehill: Writer, researcher and author of* The Soviet UFO Files *(1998) and* Paranormal Mysteries of Eurasia *(2011), and coauthor of* UFO Case Files of Russia *(2010).*

FATE July-August 2011

# Things That Fall from UFOs
## Ray Palmer

On October 24, 1957 the town of Portales in Eastern New Mexico was blanketed by mysterious cobweblike material that fell from the sky. Silk threads as long as 50 feet festooned telephone and power lines and created a nuisance in nearby corn and cotton fields where harvesting was underway.

What happened in Portales has been happening for many years, sometimes related directly to Unidentified Flying Objects and sometimes with no apparent connection.

Silk threads are undoubtedly the commonest kind of fall connected with UFOs and have been almost universally dubbed "angel hair." What is "angel hair"?

First of all, from information we are able to gather, a complete study of "angel hair" never has been made either from a viewpoint of chemical composition or from a viewpoint of location of falls.

Where does it occur, and when? Is it even possible that "angel hair" may be several different kinds of substances with several different origins?

For example, on October 4, 1957, a "tadpole-shaped" object passed over Ichinoseki City in Northeast Japan – which was the same day, coincidentally, that Russia launched its first sputnik.

As the UFO passed over the city, "angel hair" began falling, and the fall lasted from 10 AM to noon. The material consisted of threads like spiderwebs and in great profusion.

A chemical analysis of the material disclosed it to be organic, dissoluble in hydrochloric acid and inflammable. The report stated that from Roentgen photographic determinations it could not have been spiderwebs or fibers.

Careful consideration of this report discloses an apparent contradiction. First, the report says the material was organic. But then it denies that it was either spiderwebs or fibers. It seems contradictory to have determined the organic nature of the substance and then to state flatly that it was not two different kinds of organic fibers, one animal, one vegetable.

As a matter of fact, there is a good case for both spiderwebs and vegetable fibers in many "angel hair" cases. It is known that heavy batches of certain species of spiders occur at times and that they are transported on filmy webs by the wind. The same thing is true of seeds surrounded by silky threads, such as cottonwood, milkweed and the like. Nature created their fibers for wide dispersal by the wind and we ourselves have seen regular windrows of them blown by the wind into favorable traps.

At the same time, they should be easily recognizable. The spiderwebs usually have the spiders enmeshed in their silky threads, and the vegetable fibers usually have attached the seeds which they were created to disperse. It would take a pretty unobservant person, it seems to us, or unusual circumstances to confuse them.

A great deal, though not all, of the "angel hair" seems to fall in New Mexico.

Last February 21, for example, a shower of the shiny cobwebby stuff fell near Los Lunas. It looked like tinsel and collected in trees, on wires and around clothes.

On March 20, 1957, W. B. Brown, an Air Force veteran and businessman who lives at Route 3, Steel Creek, North Carolina, but works in Charlotte, saw five UFOs as he left his office with his wife after he had been working late.

*Do aliens eject their debris from UFOs?*

As the Browns watched, one of the objects separated from the other four and tumbled to the ground only 60 feet distant from the Browns. Mr. Brown approached it and said it was "foamlike but clear" with a "slimy" feel and had a cooling or numbing effect on his fingertips. Mr. Brown had a cold and was unable to detect an odor about the substance, but his wife said it smelled like burned matches or sulphur. The object seemed to melt into and soak the ground.

Could the object seen by the Browns be a kind of material that, under different circumstances, would be blown apart by winds and fall in shreds as "angel hair"? This is speculation only, but we are dealing in an area where we have so little definite factual material to go on that all we can do is speculate.

One of the most detailed cases of a web-like fall from the sky occurred in Chemung County, New York, on August 27, 1956. Charles Reese of Sagetown, about eight miles south of Elmira, left his farmhouse around 6:30 AM to do his chores. Over a two-acre chicken range he discovered thousands of bright, shiny metallic shreds scattered over the ground. They resembled the "icicles" used on Christmas trees. The material showed slight radioactivity.

Now it is a fact that a similar substance is used by military aircraft to jam radar reception. The British call this material "window" and our own Air Force calls it "chaff." When dropped from airplanes in quantity it confuses the radar sets because they pick up the reflections from the "chaff" as well as from the airplane.

The main point at which this chaff did not look like the chaff used by the Air Force is that it was silver-colored on one side and lavender tinted on the other. Officers at Griffiss Air Force Base in Rome, New York admitted that they never had seen or heard of chaff of this color. Whatever the substance was, it brings us to consider a theory that has been too long neglected.

That is, the falling material associated with so many UFO sightings may not be a byproduct of UFO propulsion but is used for the same purpose that our own Air Force uses chaff! It is well known that time after time when radar operators have locked onto a UFO it seems to disappear or fade away. At other times, even when the UFO is visually seen by observers on the ground, it is invisible on the radar screens.

Is it not at least a possibility, therefore, that UFOs use chafflike materials to make them invisible or to confuse the radar?

The only alternate theory that makes sense, considering report after report, is that UFOs are both material and immaterial; that is, capable of rendering themselves immaterial at will and hence invisible or transparent at least to radar reflections.

On the other hand, we should not forget that all kinds of things keep falling from the skies all the time. A good many of them are identifiable as familiar objects and it may be that the others are not because we don't know enough about them. The greatest mystery is still: where do they come from?

The frequent ice falls that have been going on for years, in our opinion, never have been explained. And if the theory that the ice comes from aircraft waste water is partly true, how do we explain that ice was falling before there were any airplanes to have waste water? And how do we explain the occasional concentrated and repeated falls within confined areas?

How do we explain the falls of small fish, small toads and frogs? And many other things?

Last September and October there were falls of huge pieces of a thin, clear plastic in Eastern Klickitat County, Washington. They were observed over an area covering many square miles. Deputy Sheriff George McCready found pieces on his ranch as big as 12 feet by 20 feet.

They were of varying size and could be seen all over the huge fields. One piece on another ranch was big enough to cover a stack of baled hay. The area of the fall is several miles wide and at least 15 miles long.

The material was .002 inches thick and made from strips 60 inches wide welded together. Most edges had irregular tears, although a few were torn at the seams.

It was suggested that the finds represented the remains of a balloon or balloons, but their extent would indicate a balloon of absolutely tremendous size, or many huge balloons. No one, as far as we know, made an effort to determine the number of square feet of plastic in the entire area.

Cholly Knickerbocker's column from New York last year stated that Countess Marie-Laure De Noailles heard that a UFO had landed at Hyeres on the French Riviera, near where she was staying. She hurried there and found a small piece of metal which she turned over to the French Naval laboratory at Toulon for analysis. Experts later said it was a metal they'd never seen before and that they hadn't been able to analyze it. We think this is somewhat questionable.

Then there has been a great deal of controversy over analysis of waste material supposedly dropped by three UFOs over Campinas, near São Paulo, Brazil. Most of it was seized by the Brazilian Air Force but a chemist, Dr. Risvaldo Maffei, claimed to have analyzed it and said it showed a strange alloy, with 88.91 per cent tin but without the common impurities of lead antimony, iron, etc. Our information doesn't indicate what the remaining 11.09 per cent of the alloy was.

Before we close, we ought to report that the spring of 1958 was only mildly active with UFO sightings. April and May showed some sightings, June hardly any. We are including a few representative reports.

- Six UFOs were reported over Mt. Hood, Oregon at 8:20 PM on March 10. At least seven persons reported seeing them in the Sandy Eagle Creek area. Jack R. Reef, a former communications executive of the California Eastern Aviation Company, declared the objects were flying east to west. All were lighted and gave a faint droning noise quite unlike a jet aircraft. All had white lights and if standing still could have been mistaken for a star formation except that at intervals they showed flashing red and white lights similar to regular aircraft navigation lights. They took approximately six minutes to fly from horizon to horizon.

*Author's comment: The only unusual thing about this sighting, which otherwise could be explained as a conventional military formation flight, is the droning sound of the aircraft. This has not been explained.*

- A correspondent in Phoenix, desiring to remain anonymous, reports that he has seen something very peculiar in that area – a mist "like a white cloud" changing form as it moved along, traveling from west to east at a high rate of speed.
- Near Ellwood City, Pennsylvania, just before Easter, a two-foot red blinking disc over the Walnut Ridge housing area frightened children. Police Officers Joséph Scala and Emanuel Mavero investigated and watched the bright disc for 10 minutes. They said: "At first, we thought it was an airplane or some kids with a balloon, shining a light on it. But the situation got mysterious when the radio in the police car went out of order and we could not get in touch with the department."
  
  The night was brightly moonlit, and the patrolmen could see the object rising and falling, with its light blinking. After about 10 minutes they decided to get closer to it but when they got to the top of the hill the object had disappeared.
- Anne Lesnikowski of Martha's Vineyard, Massachusetts, early in April saw a series of yellow lights low in the sky off East Chop. At first, she thought it was a ship coming into the harbor but soon saw that the lights had neither the right color nor placement and were too high on the horizon. For the first minute or so they seemed to hold their position in the sky, although oscillating slightly. Then they moved slowly toward the mainland. Four

lights went out; the other five slowly lost altitude and appeared to sink into the sea.

- A bullet-shaped lighted object flashed across southeastern states on April 20. It moved rapidly, and was fiery red with a yellow tail. It then appeared to burst with a blinding flash and two tremendous explosions.

*Author's comment: Undoubtedly a meteor.*

- A round flat object, about 45,000 feet high with green, red and white flashing lights, was seen over Houston, Texas, early on May 8. At least two police officers saw it.
- Sputnik watchers of the Jacksonville, Florida, Astronomers Club saw a bright light which appeared to be pushing a smaller, dimmer one on May 16. It moved straight across the sky to the horizon, then made a 180-degree turn, followed by another 180-degree turn. Then it disappeared. A television cameraman who photographed the UFO said it appeared to be "dumbbell shaped" on his film.
- Mysterious patches of blackened grass covering an area of over a quarter of an acre on scattered pieces of property west of Estacada, Oregon were under close observation after they were discovered to be radioactive late in May. Marion Fletcher, Route 2, Estacada, found some of the spots on his property and asserted that the blackened ground burned his finger when he touched it.

　　At first the problem was referred to the county agent's office since the blackened grass appeared to be stricken with some type of plant blight. Later it was reported that the radioactivity had disappeared and really had been negligible in the first place. The blackened blotches did not seem to follow any pattern.

- A bright, star-shaped object skimmed over the northeastern San Gabriel Valley in California for nearly an hour and a half before dawn on May 26. It did not appear to be an aircraft because of its slow speed and shape. To some it looked like a red flare. The object disappeared gradually at sunrise. It did not show up on photographic film. The night and atmosphere were clear.

These are the only reports we will have space to record in this article. The trouble with them, as with so much UFO material, is that they are not related to each other; they show no pattern. It is quite possible that they represent different types of sky objects, for we never have been adamant in believing that UFOs represent but a single type.

Because of the confusion inevitable in these separate observations, this article marks the first in a series of *interpretative analyses* of UFOs which will attempt to bring some order out of the seeming chaos and which will be published in FATE from time to time. Our interest will be less in reporting individual sightings than in trying to discern a meaningful pattern in groups of sightings. FATE hopes readers will continue to send in their individual reports; they are essential to this project.

*[Editor's Note: this article was originally published under one of Ray Palmer's pseudonyms, Robert N. Webster.]*

*Ray Palmer (1910-1977): prolific author, editor and publisher; editor of* Amazing Stories *from 1938-49; co-author with Kenneth Arnold of the book* The Coming of the Saucers; *author of numerous science fiction and fantasy stories, many written under pseudonyms; co-founder with Curtis G. Fuller of* FATE *magazine in 1948. Palmer sold his interest in* FATE *to Fuller in 1955 and went on to publish* Mystic *magazine, which became* Search.

FATE October 1958

# The Sinister Men in Black
## John A. Keel

Mysterious cameramen seem to have appeared repeatedly throughout the United States during the summer of 1967 and, according to the testimony of widely scattered witnesses, photographed the homes and families of persons who have reported close experiences with unidentified flying objects. As described, all these photographers bore a striking physical resemblance to each other. They wore the same kind of clothing and arrived in identical vehicles. Until now they have not been mentioned in any newspaper or magazine. Their identity and purposes remain unknown.

To add to the mystery, these peripatetic cameramen managed to single out people who *had not* reported their UFO experiences to any newspaper or official agency. In some cases, they had not even told their neighbors of what they had seen. Despite their total anonymity they somehow were tracked down by the "mystery men" shortly after their sightings.

As a professional reporter and fulltime UFO investigator, I have traveled many thousands of miles in the past two years and have uncovered many unusual cases which otherwise might have gone unnoticed and unrecorded. During my trips I frequently am approached by people who are afraid of publicity and hesitate to report their outlandish stories to the local authorities or to the Air Force. The misfortunes of former police officer Dale Spaur, one of the men who chased a UFO through two states in April 1966, were well-publicized (he lost his job and suffered marital troubles after his story was revealed), and few persons are willing to risk similar ridicule and anguish.

There is self-imposed censorship on the part of many UFO witnesses, which has been the biggest barrier to my investigations. I sometimes spend days, even weeks, winning the confidence of such witnesses before they break down and tell me their complete story. Often they swear me to secrecy and make me promise to keep their identity and – and in some cases – their location confidential. But I do have this full information in my files, together with tape recordings, photographs and affidavits. When I uncover *anything* in the witness's story or background which might make his or her story even slightly suspect, I file the whole case in my "Uncertain" file and omit it from my reports.

Basically, I am concerned with the "Big Picture" ... the overall situation. Each new report adds a small piece to the massive puzzle. The incredible scope and continuous activity of unidentified flying objects in many areas seems unbelievable to newcomers to the field and overwhelms even hard-core UFO buffs who have convinced themselves of the validity of the oversimplified extraterrestrial explanation.

The truth may be that "flying saucers" are merely a symptom of the problem, a diversion to distract us from the many strange things occurring at ground level and often encompassing entire communities. The activities of the "mystery photographers" may be only one aspect, which has gone completely unnoticed by UFO buffs dedicated to collecting worthless information about the altitude and speed of foreign objects observed overhead.

In previous newspaper and magazine articles I have examined at length the many stories about the "Men in Black," those mysterious and unlikely characters first introduced in Gray Barker's controversial book *They Knew Too Much About Flying Saucers*. At first, I was willing to dismiss the MIB as the paranoid fantasy of UFO cultists, but in the past year I have spoken with many persons who claimed firsthand experience

*Gray Barker's 1956 book that introduced the Men in Black.*

with these unidentified people (and who, incidentally, never had heard of Barker or his book).

For example, at 9:30 PM on the evening of September 30, 1967, I received a long-distance call from an anxious woman, the wife of a prominent politician, in New York State. This woman had called a few days before, after hearing me on a local radio program, to report a series of strange incidents involving a low-flying metal disk around her home in an isolated, wooded area. She had told her husband about it but he had refused to believe her. (Later I became quite involved in this woman's case and am convinced of her truthfulness. Her husband finally did believe her ... but that's another story.) She said that a large black car was parked directly outside her home while she was talking to me. She described the following action as it took place.

Two men got out of the car and proceeded to unlimber some kind of large camera. Both men were the same height, five feet nine inches tall, and both wore identical black suits, black turtleneck sweaters and broad-brimmed black hats. At first, she thought they were priests of some kind, but there was something about them which frightened her. Their skin was dark and their features had an Oriental cast which seemed evil to her. When they failed to approach the house but merely busied themselves with their camera, she decided to call me. (Her husband was not home at the time.) As she spoke with me and described the scene, the two men proceeded to take pictures of her house, using some kind of pale red flashgun. (Remember, it was 9:30 PM and dark ... an odd time to take pictures.) After a few minutes they closed up their camera, got into their car and drove off.

I had heard this scene described many times before. Three men dressed in this same manner had turned up in West Virginia in the summer of 1967 and had been seen by several reliable witnesses. Two such men had been observed taking photographs of the homes of UFO witnesses in broad daylight on Long Island in June. That same month I responded to a series of strange phone calls urging me to go alone to an isolated spot on a back dirt road nearby.

There I found a large black Cadillac containing two dark-skinned men in dark suits apparently waiting for me. They blinked their headlights at me and then slowly drove off. I followed them for several miles, until they went around a bend in the road in a heavily forested area and disappeared. I cruised around for several minutes trying to pick up their trail when suddenly they reappeared behind me and followed me! I stopped and started to get out of my rented car but they drove slowly on past me and again vanished.

Apparently, the whole episode was staged to convince me that the Men in Black really do exist. Their car bore no license plates. I attempted to take pictures of it but it was night and the photos did not come out.

Numerous witnesses on Long Island reported seeing the MIB and their black cars throughout the summer of 1967. In many of these cases the windows of the cars were described as totally opaque ... a dark charcoal color which made it impossible for the witnesses to see the occupants. On several occasions these cars allegedly attempted to run down witnesses walking across the street. A large black car containing two men dressed in black also came within inches of colliding with a car driven by Mrs. Mary Hyre, a reporter for the Athens, Ohio *Messenger*, in

*A Man in Black from Barker's book.*

Point Pleasant, West Virginia, in September. Mrs. Hyre has carefully and meticulously investigated and reported upon the many UFO sightings in her area during the past year.

Sixty miles north of Point Pleasant, in Parkersburg, West Virginia, a young family man from Belpre, Ohio had a brief encounter with two black-garbed, Oriental-looking men on a main street in August. He said that they appeared confused or drunk (a common description) and seemed to have difficulty walking.

When I interviewed him and his family in November, I learned that a mysterious car had pulled up in front of their home about two weeks before my visit and that a man in a black suit had apparently taken photos of their house with a large camera. Two of their neighbors also had witnessed this and corroborated their story. The unidentified photographer did not pay any attention to any of the other houses on the street.

In April, another Ohio man reported being pursued by a strange flying object while driving along Route 2 on the West Virginia side of the river. Months later, toward the end of October, he returned home from work to find a prowler in his apartment. The prowler was about five feet nine inches tall, dressed in black and carrying some kind of camera. He set off a flashgun which temporarily blinded the witness and escaped out the open door.

Individually, these stories are worthless. But I now have collected many of them from many different sections of the country, all containing the same remarkable details and all coming from ordinary, honest people who never connected these peculiar incidents with their UFO experiences. I also have made spot checks to determine if these photographers have approached non-UFO witnesses in the same areas. The results were negative.

Are these mysterious Men in Black part of a large, widespread organization engaged in obtaining information and photographs of people who have had close encounters with the UFOs?

In the majority of the cases I have investigated, such people claim they actually were pursued by the objects or were in the immediate vicinity of a brief landing or hovering operation. Since most of these people have remained voluntarily silent, as stated earlier, it is unlikely that any government agency could have known about their experiences. Indeed, my frequent visits to Washington, DC and my close liaison with numerous agencies in government have convinced me that these "mystery men" can be in no way related to the Air Force or the United States government.

The Air Force has, in fact, issued an order to all commands urging intelligence officers to be on the watch for these strangers. The MIB are openly violating several federal laws. Usually their cars do not bear any kind of license plates. In two cases in my files, the witnesses did see license plates and copied down the numbers. A police check revealed that the numbers were not in use ... such plates never had been issued! In another case, the witness reported seeing a black plate bearing a large gold "V" on the back of the car. A double "XX" also has been reported. Why haven't the police ever spotted these cars?

I've checked with the police departments in West Virginia, Ohio and Long Island where these vehicles have been seen and reported and found that no police officer has ever seen one of them.

The UFO mystery is filled with contradictions, coincidences and seemingly deliberate diversions. While it may appear the MIB are keeping careful tabs on people who have seen something special or who have been singled out by the objects (or by their occupants) for special attention, we should not overlook the possibility that these mystery men may serve no purpose other than to create side issues, to produce fear and confusion among witnesses and investigators.

We also should consider the close resemblance of the descriptions given of these men to the descriptions given of ufonauts by those who claim to have seen some. Witnesses such as John Reeves of Brooksville, Florida, Woodrow Derenberger of Mineral Wells, West Virginia and many others who have reported seeing the pilots of the "flying saucers" have described them as dark-skinned with Oriental features. In other words, do the people (?) said to be riding around in UFOs share the physical characteristics of the men riding around in black Cadillacs?

Perhaps it is time for us to reconsider the popular speculations about "flying saucers" and reexamine the somewhat baseless conclusion that they are of extraterrestrial origin. A much bigger game may be afoot here. Perhaps we have been deliberately misled into assuming they are not of this planet. There never has been any evidence, either physical or observational, to indicate that they come from elsewhere.

Actually, all the available evidence suggests that the objects are made of earthly materials and piloted by humanoid types not too dissimilar from us. We may, in fact, be dealing with a subversive group who, like the Gypsies, are able to live among us unnoticed and isolated from our general society. The UFOs may be used only to transfer these unknown people from one surface point to another. The machines themselves, if they are machines, could have been manufactured centuries ago and might emanate from hidden bases located in isolated regions scattered around this planet. Certainly the massive number of historical sightings, going back thousands of years, indicates the UFOs *always* have been a natural part of our environment.

If the Men in Black do not represent our government – and I believe that they do not – then they must come from some other secretive group or organization directly related to the UFOs. And they are successfully infiltrating our cities and villages on a large scale. When an innocent citizen accidentally learns of their presence their representatives zero in on him or her, perhaps to prepare the way to silence the witness at some point in the future. They photograph the person's home and family. In many cases, they also tap the witness's telephone and, inexplicably, even tamper with his mail.

If these many witnesses were to relate their experiences to psychiatrists, they probably would put them down as schizoid paranoiacs. It is only in the matching of the corresponding details from many such stories that we are forced to realize that we well may be dealing with something beyond an ordinary mental aberration. The late Captain Edward Ruppelt, one-time head of the Air Force's Project Blue Book, admitted that all such stories were automatically shoved into a massive "C.P." ("crackpot") file. Apparently, it never occurred to the Air Force to study its "C.P." file for corroborating details.

Recently the heavy-handed FBI moved in on three cases I had been investigating. I know they rejected one of these outright, classifying the witness – a distinguished man in his community – as a "nut."

The sober truth is that the United States government does not have any kind of law enforcement agency equipped with sufficient funds and trained personnel to investigate these matters properly. Air Force Intelligence operates on a very limited scale within the United States and it just hasn't got enough men – or enough authority – to investigate these cases. The CIA has no authority at all within the continental United States ... it is devoted primarily to the collection of information. Further handicapping possible governmental investigation is the sad fact that very few of these witnesses are willing to report their experiences directly to an official agency. In most cases they do not even talk to their local police about it.

Early in the "saucer era" (following 1947), such witnesses were exposed to so much ridicule (with their sincere letters ending up in the Air Force's "crackpot" file) that succeeding witnesses became cautious and secretive.

Adding to the dilemma, the early UFO buffs who claimed to experience telephone interference and mail tampering hurled unfounded accusations at "the government" and an anti-government attitude blossomed in UFO research circles. Gradually this attitude rubbed off on the public at large and was further increased by the Air Force's stubborn and absurd "explanations" of many outstanding UFO sightings. Today the government has been completely cut off from its chief source of UFO information – the American public.

I am sure that for every case I have uncovered there must be hundreds more that have gone unreported to anybody. The Men in Black ... whoever they are, wherever they're from ... have been able to operate with impunity, without interference, secure in the knowledge that their victims never would talk for fear of being labeled "insane," or even if they did talk, that no one would believe them.

All of the witnesses I have interviewed have told me they felt there was something inherently "evil" about these Men in Black – something alien and dangerous. In a number of cases, people apparently have been drugged or hypnotized by the MIB and several have suffered amnesia and memory lapses after alleged face-to-face confrontations.

Perhaps all of this sounds like a bad plot from *The Invaders* TV series, but it seems to be very real. Experience and many in-depth interviews with bewildered people all over this country have convinced me that this is part of the elusive "secret" behind the "flying saucers." And perhaps only a small part at that. It has been kept from you not by the Air Force or government, but by the entities behind the UFO phenomenon itself.

*John A. Keel (1930-2009): A longtime student and author of Fortean phenomena and other mysteries of existence; prolific journalist, writer and author; FATE columnist.*

FATE April 1968

# Abductions

# Kidnapped by a UFO

## Allan Spraggett

A highly respected New England couple report the most unusual and dramatic experience with a UFO on record – they claim they were abducted by one.

Their case has attracted the close attention of serious investigators, including the United States government's chief scientific consultant on UFOs, Dr. J. Allen Hynek, head of the astronomy department at Northwestern University. And, in fact, the case may have been responsible for an unpublicized visit which Dr. Hynek made to U Thant, secretary general of the United Nations, to alert him to the global nature of the UFO problem.

On September 19, 1961, Mr. and Mrs. Barney Hill, of Portsmouth, New Hampshire, encountered a huge, disk-shaped UFO at close quarters while returning from Montreal on State Route 3 near Franconia Notch, New Hampshire. They were so traumatized by the experience that they had to undergo months of hypnoanalysis at the hands of one of Boston's leading psychiatrists, Dr. Benjamin Simon.

"It had taken us four hours to negotiate a two-hour drive and this began to bother us. It was as if, somewhere along the trip, I had undergone a complete mental blackout," Mr. Hill recalls.

Under separate hypnotic treatment Mr. and Mrs. Hill penetrated this period of total amnesia which apparently lasted the two hours covering their encounter with the UFO. While hypnotized both told substantially the same story: they had been abducted by the occupants of a UFO.

They said they had been taken aboard the alien craft and subjected to a physical examination by "humanoid" beings, then released unharmed with the suggestion that they would remember nothing of what had transpired.

The Hills' story became known recently when they related it to a meeting of the New England UFO Study Group in Quincy, Massachusetts.

Then, In October 1965, a series of articles in a Boston newspaper set forth the substance of a tape recording made at that meeting.

Barney Hill told the study group that the "spaceship" was cigar-shaped, appearing as a continuous band of light when moving fast but producing a winking effect when it slowed. Two rows of lighted windows were visible along the front. There was no noise, and he and his wife saw no exhaust trail. The object first had appeared as an intense light as they traveled south and it traveled north very fast. But it changed directions abruptly and shortly thereafter was hovering over their auto.

Longtime postal employee Barney Hill said they had not told their story previously because it was too "unbelievable"!

"We stopped the car and got out to look as the object seemed to glide in our direction," he said. "At first I thought it was an airliner but suddenly it made a left turn right at us and that's when I got back inside and drove on. But the object followed us."

Mr. Hill described the object as "about as high as a 10-story building." He said the occupants "were human in form, not at all grotesque, and wearing dark, shiny jackets."

I talked with the psychiatrist who treated Mr. and Mrs. Hill, Dr. Benjamin Simon, whose professional credentials include the fact that he teaches at Tufts University medical school and is the author of two definitive psychiatric texts. Dr. Simon said that the Hills, under hypnosis, related a story of having been kidnapped by extraterrestrial beings.

*Betty and Barney Hill.*

"The Hills are above average in intelligence and emotional stability, although Barney is more sensitive than the average person," Dr. Simon said. "Both told under hypnosis what they clearly believe to be the truth. There is no question of their sincerity.

"I don't believe that they cooked up the story. Everything is against that theory. Nor do I believe they had a psychotic episode – so-called *folie de deux* – for various psychiatric reasons."

What, then, does Dr. Simon believe? That the experience actually happened to the Hills?

"The case is very intricate, very complex," he replied. "There is no way of proving they were abducted by a UFO or were not abducted. I don't believe that they were, but the Hills themselves do. To account for their strange experience, I have postulated what I call the dream hypothesis. Their experience had the qualities of a dream. From a psychiatric standpoint, it is very interesting indeed."

Dr. Simon said he believes the couple did see "some object that they took to be an extraterrestrial craft."

"I believe that what they saw probably was some atmospheric disturbance of an electrical nature," said Dr. Simon. "I do not believe in UFOs."

The psychiatrist speculates that somehow seeing this UFO unleashed tremendous anxiety which engulfed both Barney Hill and his wife simultaneously. It caused them to black out for two hours in shock. This period of amnesia was opened up under hypnosis.

"Hypnosis is the road to truth," said Dr. Simon, "but only to the truth as the subject believes it. In most cases this is also the objective truth but not always. Sometimes it is not the same as the impersonal truth, what actually happened."

However, he allowed that "there is plenty of room for different interpretations of the Hills' experience." He said that some investigators believe the couple actually were abducted by space men. Dr. Simon cited Walter Webb, a staff member of Boston's Hayden Planetarium, as one investigator who takes the Hills' story very seriously.

At first, Mr. Webb was reluctant to discuss the case when I called him. Under questioning, however, he admitted he had made a thorough investigation of the Hills' story for NICAP [National Investigations Committee on Aerial Phenomena].

"There are two parts to the Hills' experience," said Mr. Webb. "The first part is what happened before the period of amnesia. They remember seeing a huge UFO overhead, close enough that Barney could make out figures peering from the craft's windows. What they saw definitely was an unknown object.

"As to the second part of their story – well, I've heard all the tapes of the hypnotic sessions. I found no serious inconsistency in the account. There were details which were consistent with an advanced race. The story is not implausible. This case deserves to be taken seriously and should lead us to look more closely at other cases of alleged contacts by UFOs."

Mr. Webb described himself as "a firm believer" in the reality of UFOs. He believes they are extraterrestrial craft. He said he made his first personal sighting of a UFO while employed at the Smithsonian Institute tracking satellites for the United States government. His boss there was Dr. J. Allen Hynek, the government's chief UFO consultant.

Mr. Webb said that Dr. Hynek "knows that UFOs are real and he's soon going to take a tougher line on the issue."

What kind of people are Mr. and Mrs. Barney Hill?

They are respected in their community. Mr. Hill has been a leader in the New Hampshire National Association for the Advancement of Colored People (he is a Negro, his wife Betty is white). Mrs. Hill is a social worker employed by the State of New Hampshire. The Hills are in their early forties. They are members of a Unitarian-Universalist church.

"My wife and I now perceive our experience aboard the UFO as memories," Barney Hill told me, "as real as the memories I have of Philadelphia where I lived years ago. When we started treatment with Dr. Simon, he told us that hypnosis definitely was a way of getting at the truth. Now he tries to tell us that what we remember is fantasy."

Have any government officials shown interest in the Hills' story?

Mr. Hill said that a few days before November 7, 1965, when they spoke about their experience at a widely announced meeting in the Pearce Memorial Unitarian-Universalist Church in Dover, New Hampshire, two men in civilian clothes, representing themselves as insurance agents, called on the Hills. Mr. Hill said these men pumped him and his wife about their UFO encounter. Later, they discovered the men were officers from Pease Air Force Base in Portsmouth, New Hampshire.

"One man had what I thought was a bulge over his left breast," Mr. Hill said. "I believe that was a strong recording device. I noticed that this man seemed to be maneuvering around the room, but whenever he questioned me about the UFO he stood very close to me."

Mr. Hill said he and his wife are not publicity seekers. They did not speak about their experience, except to friends, for four years. Then when a Boston newspaper ran a series of articles, without their knowledge or approval, distorting the facts of their experience, Mr. Hill said he and his wife decided to set the record straight.

What do the Hills "remember" of their strange experience?

They describe the occupants of the UFO as "humanoid" and "oriental-looking." The beings, one of whom spoke English, were kind and assured the Hills they would not be harmed. They said they came from a distant planet.

One showed the Hills a "navigation chart" which Mrs. Hill later reproduced under hypnosis. (Walter Webb said this drawing was meaningless to him.)

The beings took Mr. and Mrs. Hill into separate parts of the craft, removed their clothes and subjected them to a careful physical examination.

Dr. Simon cited certain details of these physical examinations as reasons why he does not accept the Hills' story as literal truth. "The account is too bizarre," he said. "It contains many absurdities. For instance, Mrs. Hill said that the creatures inserted a needle into her navel to determine if she was pregnant. This has obvious sexual overtones in the case of a woman who has no children. But besides that, the navel is the deadest part of the human body. Wouldn't beings advanced enough that they can cross space, and humanoid themselves, know enough elementary anatomy to realize this?

"Also, they were surprised that Barney had dentures and seemed not to know what these were. They came rushing in and tried to remove Mrs. Hill's teeth, too. They asked such questions of the Hills as: What is aging? What is time? They seemed to know nothing about these subjects. This is absurd."

Dr. Simon, who is a psychoanalyst as well as a psychiatrist, interprets the Hills' experience in Freudian terms. He believes their interracial marriage was a crucial factor in the experience. As he interprets it, Barney Hill's anxiety over the interracial marriage (an anxiety which Dr. Simon says revealed itself in many ways under hypnosis) predisposed him toward some kind of emotional upheaval. He said the fact that Mrs. Hill has had no children is significant in understanding her part in the experience.

"Frankly," said Dr. Simon, "the sexual symbolism in Mrs. Hill's account is magnificent. Her story has a terrific sexual content obvious to any person who is psychoanalytically sophisticated."

What about the close harmony which existed between the stories of Mr. Hill and his wife – a harmony which could not be based on collusion since the events were shrouded in amnesia?

"Mrs. Hill had terror dreams after the encounter with the UFO," said Dr. Simon. "This was one of the symptoms that brought the Hills to me. I discovered under hypnosis that she had mentioned details of these

*Depiction of the UFO in the Hill abduction.*

dreams to Barney, although she consciously did not remember doing so. These dreams of course dealt with the alleged abduction."

Was there any physical evidence of the abduction?

Barney Hill's binocular strap was broken. His shoes were marked as though he had been in a scuffle. Also, the Hills reported that there were strange silver spots, each about the size of a quarter, on the trunk of their car. These seemed to be radioactive, and a physicist friend whom the Hills contacted by phone told them to hold a compass near the spots. When they did the needle went crazy. These spots still were visible when Walter Webb made his investigation but for some reason he did not examine them.

"I just did not think to examine the spots," Mr. Webb said when I asked him about it.

Later, the spots faded.

Dr. Simon told me that Dr. Hynek, the government's UFO expert, believed in the reality of the Hills' experience, so much so that he visited U Thant, secretary general of the United Nations, to alert him to the importance of UFO sightings.

When I talked to Dr. Hynek I asked him about these claims. He admitted going to see U Thant "on my own initiative." But he denied believing the Hills' story. "I don't believe it," he said, "although I hate to say it that bluntly."

Dr. Hynek said he went to see U Thant because "UFOs exist as a psychological reality and I wanted to alert him to the global nature of the phenomenon. UFO sightings are of considerable psychological significance. It seems to me that some dictator might be able to manipulate the emotion they arouse for his own ends."

Dr. Hynek said he does not believe that UFOs are extraterrestrial craft.

I asked, "Am I being unduly skeptical if I doubt that you went to all the trouble of seeing U Thant merely to tell him that UFOs are a psychological phenomenon, and nothing more?"

Dr. Hynek replied, "No, you would be properly skeptical. Nevertheless, I did go because I felt it was my scientific responsibility to do so."

I asked Dr. Hynek if it were true that he takes UFOs more seriously in private than his public statements would seem to indicate.

He replied, "I go so far as to say this: Any phenomenon that has been kicking around for 20 years deserves serious scientific attention. When I started investigating UFOs in 1948 I would have bet that by 1952 at the latest the whole thing would be forgotten. The persistence of the phenomenon requires careful study."

However, Dr. Hynek repeated that he does not accept the theory of extraterrestrial craft. "That's only a theory, and nothing more," he said.

Of the case of Mr. and Mrs. Barney Hill, he stated, "Some stimulus must have triggered their experience. But what that stimulus was, I don't know. I'm not a psychiatrist."

On the night Barney and Betty Hill reported encountering the UFO, there were reports of other sightings in the same area. One report said the UFO had been picked up on radar as "a shimmering mass."

The United States Air Force says what the Hills saw was a mirage produced by temperature inversion.

Dr. Simon, the psychiatrist, says they had a vivid Freudian dream.

Barney Hill and his wife say they encountered a star ship which had crossed the abyss of space, and they spent two hours on board it.

A detailed account of their strange experience will be published soon in book form by Dial Press, *The Interrupted Journey*, by John G. Fuller.

*Allen Spraggett: Writer and religion editor for* The Toronto Star *and host of the radio show* The Unexplained.

FATE January 1967

# An Alien Heat: Chronicles of Sex and Saucery
## Scott Corrales

It is an unquestionable fact that sex has played a pivotal role in a number of UFO cases and has become the mainstay of the abduction phenomenon, whose literature centers around the non-consensual aspect of these goings-on. But these are merely the latest facet of a phenomenon that goes back to the very start of human history and myth. Who can forget the Greek gods and the numerous guises they assumed to seduce humans?

But the Mediterranean cultures were hardly alone in their beliefs. Hindu deities were equally proficient at seduction: the *Bhaghavata Purana* tells us of the exploits of the divine Krishna with mortal milkmaids. Hardly a culture in the Americas lacks a story concerning a sky maiden who fell to earth, married a mortal, and then returned to her people after having had offspring.

The notion of sexual congress has also played heavily in science fiction and other speculative writing as far back as Edgar Rice Burroughs's John Carter of Mars stories, where the human hero fights all manner of alien beings on the Red Planet and wins the affections of the alien princess Deja Thoris. (Burroughs's Martians were oviparous, so in the course of time, we can imagine that Carter's alien lover laid an egg.)

**The case to end all cases**
Many researchers and writers have agreed that were it necessary to sum up ufology in a single case, the one involving the strange experience of Brazilian farmer Antonio Villas Boas [referred to in this article as AVB] would more than likely be the one to choose.

Veteran Brazilian ufologist Fernando Cleto reminisces about the surreal days of this most unusual case: "Being a friend of João Martins, I already knew enough about the event in his own words. On one occasion, I read letters written by Villas Boas and even managed to see a small model of the 'flying saucer' and of one of its occupants – small rustic statuettes whittled out of wood by Villas Boas himself. I also recall that João Martins was completely opposed to making this case known to the public, for which reason it was disclosed much later .... after DNA. Irene Granchi disclosed the case overseas, I published my own opinion in this regard in a Belgian or British magazine – I can't remember which. I made an observation which greatly favored the Villas Boas case."

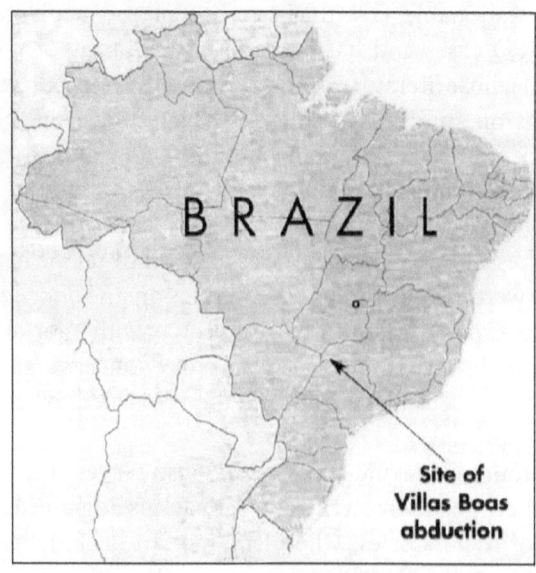
Site of Villas Boas abduction

As if the incredible AVB required any further bolstering, Fernando Cleto managed to show that there had indeed been sightings of the same elongated oval vehicle elsewhere in Brazil prior to the date of the events in the AVB case. "I remember," says Cleto, "that a few days prior to October 15, 1957, there was a case in the interior of the State of Goias. A car was forced off the roadway by a force issuing from a 'flying saucer.' The driver described something which bore a strong connection to what Villas Boas had seen. He compared the UFO to a helicopter, at first, with the power to exert traction ... and to have seen occupants similar to those seen by Villas Boas."

There is no doubt that on November 6, 1957, Colonel Ivo Gastaldoni, who was on the way to the hospital to see his newly born daughter, was summoned by his command to see a UFO hovering directly over the Cumbica Air Base. The colonel remarked that the object was high up in the air and well out of the reach of the base's fighters. His overall impression was that it resembled some sort of eggshaped craft with a helicopter blade spinning over the ovoid fuselage.

"The event with the driver before October 15, 1957, when added to the November 6 case," writes Cleto, "coincided with the description given by Villas Boas for his own object and impressed me greatly. It was as if a certain model of UFO carrying a very special crew complement had been operating in a given region of Brazil for a given period of time while on a special mission."

Ufologist Cleto notes in his memorandum regarding the AVB case that João Martins' reluctance to disclose the particulars of the astonishing event was to keep mentally unbalanced individuals from conjuring up similar scenarios.

### The AVB episode

But what exactly happened to Antonio Villas Boas?

The deposition taken by investigator Dr. Olavo T. Fontes and subsequently delivered to Brazil's Ministry of the Navy remains the cornerstone of research into the case. It was taken in Fontes' office on February 22, 1958 and witnessed by journalist Martins himself.

Villas Boas began by stating that he was 23 years old at the time and was a farmer by profession. He lived on a *fazenda* [estate or large farm] on the outskirts of Sao Francisco de Sales, Minas Gerais, not far from São Paulo, and came from a large family composed of two brothers and three sisters who all lived in the immediate area. The young farmer explained that it was their custom to work two shifts during the planting season: one at night, which he was responsible for, and another by day which was handled by farm hands.

On October 5, 1957, Villas Boas went to bed at 11 PM following a party at the farmhouse. He shared the room with his younger brother, João, and they were both witnesses to a strange nocturnal light which lit up the entire room and had its source in one of the animal pens on the farm.

It was 10 days later on October 15 that Antonio Villas Boas would have his historic experience. While driving his tractor, he noticed a shining star that increased in brightness as if descending to earth. "In a matter of seconds," he told his interviewers, "it turned into a very shiny oval object headed straight for me." He tried to escape from it by speeding up the tractor, but the object had already landed some 10 to 15 meters ahead of the tractor. "It got closer and I was able to see, for the very first time, that it was a strange device with a slightly rounded shape, encircled by small lights and with a large, enormous red light in front, from which came all the light I could see when it was higher ... the machine's shape was now clearly visible. It resembled a large, elongated egg with three spurs in front." AVB added the curious detail that "something appeared to be spinning at high speed on top of the vehicle and gave off a reddish fluorescent light."

## The abduction

Seized by terror, Antonio jumped off the tractor in hopes of eluding his pursuers on foot, but the furrowed terrain made a speedy getaway impossible. The next thing he knew, someone had seized him by the arm. It was a figure much shorter than he, wearing a "strange outfit" and a helmet. The farmer pushed the figure away and managed to knock it to the ground, but three more similarly dressed figures turned up, seizing him by his arms and legs, and bore him off to the waiting craft.

Villas Boas indicated that he did not go off meekly to whatever fate awaited him: he kicked, screamed and hurled insults at his helmeted captors. Given the narrowness of the vehicle's access stairway, the farmer managed to break away from his captors, but he was overpowered once more by their uncanny strength and superior numbers.

The humanoids dragged him into the craft, where he was stripped naked and subjected to several indignities. His captors drew a blood sample from his chin using a chalice-like device, and after slathering him with a strange liquid that covered his entire body, he was taken to a room – unfurnished but for a couch – where he was left alone for some 20 minutes, by his count. At this point, a mixture of fear, nausea and coldness, coupled to the stench of a strange gas that was pumped into the room, led him to vomit in one of the corners.

"After a long time," Villas Boas said, "a noise at the door startled me. I turned in that direction and was shocked to see that it was now open and a woman was entering the room, walking toward me. She was approaching slowly, perhaps amused at the astonishment that must have been visible on my face.

"My jaw had dropped and with good reason. This woman was completely naked, as was I, and barefoot. She was also pretty, although different from the women I'd known. Her hair was an almost whitish shade of blonde, as if peroxided, straight and not very abundant, neck-length and with the ends curled inward. Her eyes were blue and large, more narrow than round and slanted outward – like the pencil-painted eyes of those girls who fancy themselves Arabian princesses and make their eyes look slanted; that's what they were like. Only it was a completely natural effect, since there was no paint at all involved."

The strange liquid which had been spread over his body, apparently some sort of aphrodisiac, began to work. Antonio felt less tense as the small woman began to caress him, ultimately seducing him.

"It sounds incredible," he confessed to Fontes and Martins during the interview, "given the situation I was in. I believe that the liquid they rubbed on me was the cause of it. All I know is that I felt an uncontrollable sexual excitement, which had never happened to me before. I forgot about everything and held the woman, returning her caresses with my own.

"We ended up on the couch, where we had relations for the first time. It was a normal act and she responded like any woman. Then came a period of more caressing followed by more sexual relations. In the end, she was tired and breathing quickly. I was still excited, but she now refused and tried to get away. When I noticed that, I cooled down too. That was what they wanted from me, a good stallion to improve their stock."

The door opened once more and two of the "crewmen" appeared, summoning the woman away. Before leaving, she turned to the farmer and pointed at her belly, then pointing at him, and finally at the heavens. Curiously, Villas Boas took this to mean that "she would return to take me from where it was she came."

## Dismissed

After having served as breeding stock, Antonio was unceremoniously led off the vehicle, which took off immediately. Returning to his tractor, Villas Boas learned that the time was now 5:30 in the morning. Estimating that it had been around 1:15 AM when he was abducted, his entire experience had lasted some four hours and 15 minutes.

"My mother told me I shouldn't become involved with those people again. I didn't have the courage to tell my father, since I had already told him about the light that appeared over the pens, and he didn't believe me, telling me that I was seeing things …" Villas Boas concluded.

After his traumatic experience, Villas Boas withdrew from public life to pursue his studies, earning a law degree and becoming a practicing attorney in the city of Formosa, Goias, while running a small business on the side. He died in late 1992 in the city of Uberaba, in Brazil's Triangulo Minero.

In June 1993, the late Dr. Walter K. Buhler, president of the Sociedade Brasileira de Estudos Discos Voadores (SBEDV), disclosed the fact that between 1962 and 1963, his organization had received an anonymous letter from the US inviting Villas Boas to visit this country in order to examine a recovered flying saucer in the possession of the American military. This letter was sent to Formosa, State of Goias, by Dr. Buhler. Allegedly, Villas Boas's son advised him that his father had indeed visited the United States to inspect the object but had kept silent the rest of his life concerning the visit.

## In the wake of AVB

On March 3, 1978, in the small hours of the morning, 18-year-old Jose Inacio Alvaro, studying to be an electrician at a vocationaltech [school] in the Brazilian town of Pelotas, noticed a strange glow pouring in through one of the windows of his house. Alvaro, who had been up at that late hour studying, felt an unusual torpor seize him at the very moment that a thin blue beam appeared out of the light. The next thing he remembered was waking up on the street at a considerable distance from his home. Casting a frightened look at his wristwatch, Jose Inacio realized the time was now four o'clock in the morning: he had no recollection of what events had transpired in the intervening two hours.

Jose Inacio's case attracted the attention of Brazilian ufologists who urged him to undergo hypnosis. The sessions were conducted by a number of faculty members of the University of Pelotas and at one point even included the college's chancellor.

Under hypnosis, Jose Inacio recounted an experience that rivaled the classic Antonio Villas Boas case: at a given point, he found himself in an unfurnished, circular room and in the company of a naked, dark-haired woman that was much taller than he. At that point, the student realized that he, too, was unclothed. The woman approached him, placed a hand on his forehead, and told him not to be frightened since no harm would befall him. She immediately began caressing Jose Inacio, who at first had misgivings about the situation but eventually relented. They ended up having sexual intercourse on a structure that he described as "a net."

The details of his carnal experience were intensely graphic. The hypnotists' report states that the subject's words and movements clearly indicate he was reliving the experience under trance. For the sake of decorum, the researchers allegedly erased the recording of the session.

Unlike the AVB case, there were witnesses to Jose Inacio's return from his odyssey. One resident of Pelotas claimed having seen the student lying on the street at that time of the morning; upon approaching to offer assistance, the good Samaritan alleged that Jose Inacio stood up like an automaton and began to walk away from the scene. Other local residents claimed to have witnessed the passing of a disk-shaped flying object in the air above Pelotas that caused disruptions to the power grid as it passed overhead.

The experiences of AVB and Jose Inacio Alvaro were not to be unique: theirs would soon have to share the spotlight with those of a third Brazilian man by the name of Juan Valerio.

On the evening of November 30, 1982, Juan Valerio da Silva went out of his house in the rural town of Botucatu to get some water and did not re-enter the structure. Three hours later, he was found unconscious in his backyard, naked and covered in what appeared to be oil.

Having no conscious recollection of what happened during the 12-hour absence, hypnosis was again employed to ascertain his whereabouts during the "missing time" period. Valerio claimed that he was taken to a strange place by unseen captors, stripped of his clothing, and placed beside a dark-skinned, naked woman with long black hair who forced him to engage in sexual activity. A series of "strange tattoos" were etched upon his body.

While lacking the lurid descriptions that made his predecessors' experiences famous, the importance of Valerio's story lies in what we could term the postscript: the abductee developed a number of psychic abilities, most notably telekinetic powers. He has also had repeated visits from his nonhuman hosts, and was led to believe that his eldest son, Reginaldo, was also the product of genetic experimentation by these alien entities.

### The events at Mirassol

Mirassol is a city of some 32,000 inhabitants in the state of São Paulo, Brazil. It has earned its place in ufological history due to the events which allegedly took place there in 1979. Antonio Carlos Ferreira, who was 21 years old at the time and working as a watchman for a large furniture manufacturer in town, had his own experiences with nonhuman entities.

At three o'clock in the morning on June 28 of that year, Ferreira witnessed a large, shining light descend from the darkness onto the ground not far from where he stood watch. As he concentrated on the bright light, he then noticed that three diminutive entities were approaching. Their heads were covered by opaque helmets and their bodies were encased in form-fitting suits with what the young watchman took to be "breathing devices." Before Ferreira knew it, one of the beings fired a beam of red light that left him paralyzed. Then he was conveyed – in this state of immobility – toward the painfully bright light, which turned out to be a small, disk-shaped craft that shuttled Ferreira and his captors to a larger vehicle in space.

Once aboard this craft, the frightened watchman was surprised to notice two different types of nonhuman beings milling about: one had dark skin and curly red hair, and the other had lighter complexion and straight black hair. Both species had large, slanted eyes; wide mouths with thick lips; well-defined chins; and a lack of eyebrows or eyelashes.

His own abductors proved to be some sort of "mechanical men" who returned to their stations against a wall after delivering their captive.

Had nothing else occurred, Antonio Carlos Ferreira would have merely been a South American Travis Walton – a stranger in a strange place filled with nonhuman entities. But the most harrowing part of his unearthly experience was still to come. The humanoids gave the watchman multiple assurances by telepathic means that he would be returned home unharmed. Then they transferred him to a small room and told him to lie down on a couch.

## She's too repulsive for me

Feeling more at ease, Ferreira complied. Then another being appeared in the room. It was a naked female of the darker-skinned alien species. Under the hypnotic regression performed by the late researchers Walter K. Buhler, Guillermo Pereira, and Ney Matiel, Ferreira described his would-be sex partner as downright repulsive, having an unpleasant breath, an overly large chin, small breasts, and icy cold skin. The detail of red pubic hair, which had first emerged in the Villas Boas case, resurfaced in Ferreira's experience.

A struggle with the aliens – also reminiscent of the AVB case – took place as three of the creatures tore his clothes off to prepare him for the act. Ferreira was outraged and told the female not to come closer, since "her ugliness was repulsive." A slightly taller alien gave Ferreira an injection that caused him to lose strength and brought his combativeness to an end. They then covered him in a dark, amber-colored oil and placed the repulsive-looking female on top of him. The sexual act was rapidly consummated, and the aliens fussed over him again, bathing him in the strange oil once more. His captors informed him they came from "another planet" and that their mission was to secure human offspring for future research. He was told that he would be contacted once more in order that he could meet his hybrid offspring.

At one point, Ferreira complained of an inability to breathe, and his abductors gave him an unpleasant-tasting liquid that appeared to remedy the situation. Similar "cordials" (for want of a better word) have also been described in other Brazilian cases, such as the one involving the soldier "Jose Antonio" who was abducted by strange dwarves while fishing on a riverbank.

Ferreira apparently underwent other abduction events of which he had no conscious recollection whatsoever – the second in January 1983 and the third in April of that same year.

## One day while chasing kites

This case takes us from equatorial Brazil to the Caribbean, where in 1934, a teenager identified only as "Julio" became the protagonist of an episode that would scar him for life. It was first investigated by Puerto Rican ufologist Sebastian Robiou (mid-1970s), then re-investigated by Salvador Freixedo (late 1980s). The witness has since been interviewed once more by Magdalena del Amo-Freixedo (1997).

One morning, while flying a brand new kite on a slope outside the city of Mayaguez, Puerto Rico, before going off to school, young Julio was startled to see his kite being sucked in by what appeared to be an air pocket or vacuum of some kind. He pulled on the string and noticed an inordinate amount of resistance from the wayward kite. Upon looking up, he was amazed to see a ball "like a ball bearing," but measuring some 20 feet across and having the same coppery hue of a BB. A light issued from the object, and he felt himself being raised into the air. Before he knew it, he was inside the strange flying object.

"On one side, I saw a girl," Julio indicated during the interview conducted by Robiou, "and on the other was a guy looking at some sort of giant emerald. He wore a tight-fitting, olive-drab suit that looked like plastic. I couldn't see his face, because he was minding the device. He gestured at the girl... The girl had a pinkish complexion and wore a silvery suit. She was small, like one of our six-year-old girls, with platinum blonde hair. I don't remember the color of her eyes."

Julio explained that the child was holding his kite in her hands, and that he made all possible efforts to tell her that it belonged to him. The girl not only did not surrender the kite, but instead gave him a small box from which images could be made to appear. He did not remember how, but the object returned him to the place from which he had been collected and dumped him abruptly to the ground. He suffered a sprained ankle as a result of the experience – but he had the curious little box with him.

Further details would emerge during Freixedo's re-opening of the case. Julio, now a hardened man in his early 60s, informed the Spanish ufologist of the ultimate fate of the little box he'd been entrusted with.

The box was a 20-centimeter cube, and when its user placed his or her hands upon it, a "kind of vapor made up of lights" would spin on its surface, causing an entity – a small ape-like creature no more than a meter tall – to appear in the room. According to Julio, the entities materialized in such a manner would not speak and appeared to be surprised to find themselves in an alien environment. The girl-child on the strange object had successfully caused the "little apes" to return to their native surroundings, or "back into the box," as Julio put it.

Only the hapless boy was not so good at this final aspect. The diminutive simians would materialize and then vanish at breathtaking speed out the window, many times in the presence of his classmates who had asked him to perform the "neat trick" with the box. The apported entities were not at all pleased, claimed Julio, with their new condition. They would frighten children and dogs and appeared to prowl the surroundings of Julio's family home. "Believe me," he told the researcher, "I would just like to die. I'm tired of seeing strange things." The supernatural primates had apparently been the source of a number of mysterious deaths that had occurred in his corner of southwestern Puerto Rico over the decades.

When Magdalena del Amo-Freixedo re-opened the case as part of her book *Abducciones* (Bell Book, 1998), a further wrinkle appeared which has a direct bearing to this article.

### They meet again

Now willing to go on the record by his real name – Juan Rivera Feliberti – he explained to Del Amo-Freixedo that his contact with the alien "girl" had not stopped after the incident of the wayward kite. Many years later, now a married man with children, the experiencer moved from Mayaguez to Sabana Grande. He took his family to the beach one day. While the children frolicked in the water, "Julio" decided to go fishing. He suddenly realized he was not alone: a beautiful woman had appeared right in front of him. A wave of remembrances washed over him as he realized her blonde hair was identical to that of the girl in the odd circular vehicle so many years before. He asked her where she came from, and she allegedly replied, "From far away, from the stars ..."

Male figures soon appeared, clad identically to the one he remembered seeing back in 1934. "They were the lady's companions...

They were identical to the one I'd seen as a boy. Suddenly, I don't know what she did, but she was completely naked. She didn't tell me anything, but I understood in my mind that she wanted to have relations with me. I didn't want to... I wanted to run away. Besides, my wife could catch me if she happened to come around."

Although hesitant to describe his unusual experience to a female investigator, Del Amo-Freixedo eventually convinced him to elaborate. Uncomfortably, "Julio" continued the story: "Look, I didn't want to at first, but you know how it is. I was young and the woman was very good looking. She began caressing me all over, and we ended up like men and women do when they're both unclothed."

"Julio" bashfully added that his alien lover's body was not exactly like that of a human female: her breasts appeared to be placed lower on the torso and her pubic area was hairless. He made the curious observation that her skin, while soft, was somewhat scaly. These anatomical differences did not deter him, however: "We [had sex] several times. I think four. Back then one was full of energy and recovered quicker." In subsequent years, he would return to the scene of the events in hope of seeing his unusual sex partner again, but he never did.

As if to bring the events in the long, strange life of Juan Rivera Feliberti to a full circle, at around 3 AM one day in 1995, he saw the same girl who'd stolen his kite once more, standing outside his house.

## Things to learn

Regardless of whatever stance we may have regarding the UFO phenomenon, and if we are willing to suspend disbelief, the information which can be gleaned from these cases is of considerable interest. Absent from the scene are the greys, reptoids, and Nordics who seem to populate the abductee chronicles. Instead, we have beings of an entirely different taxonomy engaged in an operation or mission that appears to be taking place largely within the confines of Brazil. The commonalities of the experiences – the oily liquid applied on the abductees, which serves as antiseptic and aphrodisiac at once; the beverage that relieves human discomfort; the choice of intercourse rather than artificial insemination – link them together while separating them from the coldly clinical abduction phenomenon in the northern hemisphere.

The fact that this libidinous aspect of the UFO phenomenon appears to have a strong preference for Brazil has led to jocose comments on the appeal of Brazilian virility to non-human intelligences. The fact remains that somewhat similar situations have occurred elsewhere in the world – and in our own country as well.

In October 1974, oil worker Carl Higdon took a day off from work and went hunting near Rawlins, Wyoming. Coming across an elk (an astonishing piece of luck in itself on the first day of hunting), Higdon pulled the trigger on his rifle only to see the bullet issue from the weapon in slow motion and land 50 feet away from him.

To his astonishment, the hunter realized that time was standing still all around him and that a chinless, jawless alien being was looking at him. Higdon was apparently abducted and hooked up to strange devices aboard "a cube-shaped UFO." The hunter attributed the reason for his return to Earth by his captors was that he had had a vasectomy performed a few years before the abduction and was therefore useless for the "breeding program" that his captors appeared to be pursuing.

*Scott Corrales: Frequent contributor to* FATE, *and editor of* Inexplicata: The Journal of Hispanic Ufology.

FATE July 2002

# Alien Abduction Workload
## Robert J. Durant

**Introduction**

Abductions – whatever their real nature – have a history measured at least in decades and have touched a multitude of humans. The abduction experience consists of a temporary encounter with alien life.

The aliens do all the work. They initiate the event and carry out each step from the capture to the return. This involves a lengthy series of activities carried out within the framework of required results and a limited and prescribed methodology. In the following remarks I attempt to analyze the purported alien abductions in the prosaic terms of industrial workload analysis.

Simply put, how many aliens are required to accomplish the abduction? The approach will be that of a manager attempting to estimate the staffing required to manufacture a product or deliver a service. The same shop floor parameters that would be relevant to a shoe factory or a medical facility ought to apply equally in the case of an alien abduction program carried out on a host planet. The analysis that follows will assume ordinary industrial considerations, and it will assume that abductions are real physical events, systematically carried out by a large work force.

## The job

The aliens themselves have commented on the prosaic industrial constraints under which they labor. Note, for example, this exchange that Betty Hill had with an alien: "So I said, 'What are you doing with Barney? Bring him in here where I am.' And the man said, 'No, we only have equipment enough in one room to do one person at a time. And if we took you both in the same room, it would take too long.'"

This alien spokesman is not invoking magic. He has a job to do, a limited number of helpers, and a time limit. In a review of the abduction literature, folklorist Dr. Tom Bullard identified the broad outlines of the abduction job. Like all other writers on the subject, his vantage is that of the human experiencer. Luckily, what happens to the experiencer is exactly what the alien work force must get done. In a word, their job description. Other authors, notably professor David Jacobs, have produced detailed step by step accounts of the typical abduction. I quote Bullard because his data is so well organized and based on a review of all available cases as of June 1987.

According to Bullard, "Eight possible episodes comprise the abduction story: (1) Capture, (2) Examination, (3) Conference, (4) Tour, (5) Otherworldly Journey, (6) Theophany, (7) Return, and (8) Aftermath." Viewed from the perspective of the alien supervisor, this is a complicated and serious set of tasks. As we shall see, Betty Hill's informant had good reason to complain, because all this work must be done in a short time.

## Prevalence of abductions

Dr. John Miller estimates the lifetime prevalence of abductions as either 100,000 or 200,000 persons in the US, using what he terms as "two sets of crude data." His study is unique in that it is based on epidemiological grounds. He began with the number of known abduction cases and extrapolated that figure to the general population.

A number of other polls have been taken to estimate the incidence of the abduction experience. Unlike Miller's work, these rely on self-reporting via questionnaire. The questions asked are designed

*How many aliens are abducting humans?*

to count symptoms commonly thought to be indicative of abductions. An *Omni* magazine survey indicated that six percent of the population, or 15 million Americans, are abductees. Jacobs reports a survey that he conducted among students at Temple University yielded 5.5 percent. The Roper poll [1992] surveyed 6,000 adult Americans and found that two percent replied positively to four or more of the "trigger" questions. This percentage translates into 3.7 million adults, and about five million of the total (all ages) population.

The Roper survey is by far the most comprehensive, but it tells us only how many adults report symptoms associated with abductions. It can be argued that this is nothing more or less than the same diagnostic criteria used in personal investigation by abduction researchers, but it does raise problems of interpretation.

For instance, 20 percent reported waking up "...paralyzed with the sense of a strange figure or presence in the room." Taken alone as a criterion, this would mean that 50 million persons have been abducted. In the analysis that follows, however, I will use the conservative figure of five million abductees, in consonance with the interpretation of the Roper data urged by researcher Budd Hopkins, Professor Jacobs and sociologist Ron Westrum.

## Incidence of abductions

How often is the typical experiencer abducted? Multiple abductions are definitely the rule, but I have found no data in the literature with respect to the average number of abduction events over a lifetime or any specific period of time. A figure of 10 seems consistent with hints in the available data and may actually be too small. Though arbitrary, it will serve for our purposes.

## Useful lifetime

There is a parameter I call the "useful lifetime" of an abductee. The data shows abductions beginning in early childhood. According to Hopkins, "An individual, male or female, is first abducted as a child, at a time possibly as early as the third year." And in another passage, "It appears that most UFO abductees have had more than one such experience, their first abduction generally occurring in childhood around the age of six or seven."

Bullard tells us, "Abductions are a peril of youth. If you once pass 30 without ever being abducted, you have little to worry about. A periodicity shows up in the age distribution with peaks at age seven, again at 12-13, 16-17 and 20, lending support to the possibility that the captors keep tabs on a subject over the years."

At what age do abductions cease? According to Bullard, "The range of abductions is lifelong, from infancy to age 77, but the frequency plunges in a striking way after 30." I have not found a citation for this, but it is my impression that the accepted opinion has it that abductions rarely occur beyond approximately 55 years of age. This is one of the reasons given by Hopkins and Jacobs, for believing that sexual reproduction is a primary objective of the abduction process.

I will assign a value of 50 years to the "useful lifetime" parameter. In other words, the assumption is that abductions typically begin at the age of five and end at the age of 55. The statistical loading of events, such as before or after 30, is not important to our workload analysis. It will be assumed that abductions are evenly distributed throughout the useful lifetime of the experiencer.

## Duration of procedure

According to Hopkins, a typical abduction requires about two hours to accomplish: "Though the vast majority – probably more than 90 percent – of all abductions last not more than two hours, there are a few dramatic exceptions. Travis Walton, for example, was missing for a five-day period." Writing 11 years earlier in his seminal work *Missing Time*, Hopkins had this to say about a typical abduction: "What they are not aware of is that it is now two hours later."

Jacobs says this about missing time, which he and most researchers equate with the abduction process: "Missing time episodes are common in abductees' lives. They are unable to account for a 'lost' period of time, which might be as short as an hour or two or as long as a day – and sometimes even longer. Trying to understand the origin of the missing time can torture the victims. It makes no sense. They have no explanation, and yet they know it happened."

The cover of the Berkeley Medallion paperback of Fuller's *Interrupted Journey* [about the Hill abductions] proclaims in large red letters that "Hypnotism Uncovers the Awesome Secret of 2 Hours Lost From A Couple's Life!"

Barney Hill is quoted about his fateful drive from Canada: "Even if I allowed more time than I know we took at those roadside stops, there still were at least two hours missing out of that night's trip." Benjamin Simon, MD, the original abduction regression hypnotist, allowed that his patients, Betty and Barney Hill, "... were constantly haunted by a nagging anxiety centered around this period of several hours ..."

In sum, the consensus seems to favor not much more, not much less, than two hours. The alien workers would be required to perform additional tasks before and after the abduction, much as a worker in any earth-bound trade, craft or profession does. Thus, the two-hour figure seems reasonable and conservative. To perform 2,740 abductions, each taking two hours, requires 5,480 procedure-hours per day.

## Aliens per abduction

Finally, we must know how many aliens it takes to perform an abduction.

Benjamin Simon asked Barney Hill how many men were in the party that flagged down his car, and Barney replied: "I thought I saw a cluster of six men. Because three of them came to me, and three did not." However, Barney's drawing of the capture scene shows 10 dots, each meant to represent an alien.

Budd Hopkins was asked, "How many aliens are usually involved?"

Hopkins replied, "Not a lot of beings. Two or three to take the victim out of the house or car, and four or five on the ship, in the examining room. You don't run into more than six or seven in the whole business."

Division of labor on the craft is puzzling. We know that there are supervisors, and we are well aware of the aliens who assist in the examinations. But do these workers scurry from one abductee to another? Do the same workers capture and examine and then do duty in the nursery? Is there a set of pilots or maintenance men or accountants?

Every human enterprise has a very substantial portion of its work force engaged in administrative or support activity, and it seems reasonable to suppose that the aliens have an equivalent, especially in an expeditionary force presumably very far from home. Abductees would never see these workers.

We will tentatively accept six as the number of aliens involved in any given abduction.

## Preliminary computations

We have five million abductees, each experiencing 10 abductions per 50-year lifetime, for a total of 50 million abductions over that period of time, or one million per year, or 2,740 abductions per day.

Six aliens comprise an abduction team. At two hours per abduction, a team can do 12 procedures in a 24-hour day.

The number of teams required is 2,740 divided by 12, which equals 288 teams, or a total of 1,370 aliens.

This is the number of aliens required to handle only the US, assuming that the teams work without rest throughout the 24 hours, and without significant other impediments. It also ignores at least several other factors that bear mentioning.

First, abductions – like UFO sightings – are not evenly distributed throughout the 24 hours of the day. They appear to be quite predominantly a night-time activity. Any deviation from even distribution throughout the day will add to the required number of crews. For example, if two-thirds of all abductions take place during any given eight-hour period, the minimum number of required crews increases from 228 to 457.

Second, neither humans nor domesticated working animals can labor continuously, but continuous activity is assumed in these calculations. Jacobs sums up the suspicions of many researchers when he asks if at least the shorter grays might not be robots or quasi-biological entities.

They don't seem to breathe, there are no recreation or rest facilities on the craft, and no alien has ever been observed in what could be described as even a moment of rest or leisure. If, like humans in the industrialized countries, they work an eight-hour day, the number of crews required rises by a factor of three. If they are robots, even machinery needs occasional maintenance or replacement.

Assuming that there is something to the Roswell and Kecksburg cases, alien technology is far from perfect. Obviously, these are all factors requiring additional personnel and craft.

The most "magical" aspect of this operation is the assumption that the alien craft can relocate at relativistic speed, darting back and forth to capture and return their prey, but the sudden appearance and disappearance of UFOs is a commonly reported characteristic.

Granting that this discussion could go on forever, it does seem that a figure on the order of 500 crews, each consisting of six aliens, could do the job. This is a total of 3,000 aliens. It may be useful to compare this figure with the manning of naval vessels. Aircraft carriers have a crew of 5,500, and the newest destroyers carry a complement of 366.

If the abduction phenomenon is indeed worldwide, the numbers for the US must be multiplied by 22. The population ratio is 250 million versus 5.5 billion.

## Conclusion

I have made an effort to present the data clearly, drawing from authorities whenever possible and providing a simple format to enable the reader to do his own calculations in each separate parameter.

The issue really is, can abductions be physical events? With publication of the Roper Poll data, a number of researchers recoiled, thinking that five million abductees was, on the face of it, a number so large as to be incompatible with the concept of "real" abductions.

Dennis Stacy spoke for many when he wrote the following about the Roper data: "Moreover, these numbers apply only to a target American population of 185 million. If we are to assume that one in every 50 people on a planet with a population of several billion has actually been abducted at one time or another, we are now looking at a potential body-count of some several hundred millions.

"The logistics of an ongoing extraterrestrial invasion on that kind of scale simply won't compute. If true, in fact, the Earth's skies would literally be darkened with abducting UFOs day and night; they would be stacked up over the major metropolitan areas in the same way that our own 747s now crowd the air lanes over New York ... But if millions of flying saucers aren't involved in the abduction experience, what is?"

But the logistics do compute, if only we will bother to do the computing. Nor need the skies be darkened, because millions of flying saucers are not required in order to support the level of alien intervention implied by the Roper data.

*Robert J. Durant (1938-2014): Airline pilot, UFO researcher, writer, actor and close encounter experiencer at age 14.*

FATE September 1993

# Science, Religion and Metaphysics

# Open Letter to *Science*
## J. Allen Hynek

1 August 1966
The Editors of *Science*
Washington, DC

Dear Sirs:

To the best of my knowledge, the term UFO (Unidentified Flying Object) never has figured in the pages of *Science* (many might say "disfigured" the pages of *Science*). Yet some 20 years after the first public furor over UFOs (called "flying saucers" then), reports of UFOs continue to accumulate at a rate much greater than in the early days of the "craze." Just of late there has been a spate of books and articles on the subject and public interest is again rising. The newspaper and TV coverage of the recent Michigan "swamp gas" cases was widespread (and the cause of no little discomfiture to me – I have been told that the press conference was the largest in the history of the Detroit Press Club). This is a disturbing phenomenon to many, yet formal science has taken no note whatever of it.

I have been associated with the UFO phenomenon for many years as scientific consultant to the Air Force. Since the Air Force now has acted on the recommendation of myself and others to give increased scientific attention to the UFO phenomenon, I feel under some obligation to report to my scientific colleagues, who could not be expected to keep up with so seemingly a bizarre field, the gist of my experience in "monitoring the noise level" over the years in my capacity as scientific consultant. In doing so I feel somewhat like a traveler to exotic lands and far-away places who discharges his obligation to those who stayed at home by telling them of the strange ways of the natives. To carry the analogy a bit farther, it has come to my attention rather forcibly through correspondence and personal contact, that many of my colleagues in various fields are more than just a little interested in the "natives," although they might well disclaim this interest if challenged. I certainly would not have expressed openly any such interest had I not been asked to do so officially many years ago, first under "Project Sign" and later under "Project Blue Book."

During my long period of association with the reports of strange things in the sky, I expected that each lull in the receipt of reports signaled the end of the episode, only to see the activity renew; in just the past two years it has risen to a new high. Each wave of sightings adds to the accumulation of both the misidentifications of otherwise familiar things (still the great majority) and to the reports which, by present methods of attack, defy analysis. All this has increased my own concern and sense of personal responsibility and motivated me to urge the initiation of a meaningful scientific investigation of the UFO phenomenon by physical and social scientists. I had guardedly raised this suggestion in the past (*Journal of Science and Arts*, 43, 311, 1953) and at various official hearings, but with little success. UFO was a term that called forth buffoonery and caustic banter; hence no scientist would look at it. It remained a topic for buffoonery and caustic banter precisely because scientists paid no attention to the raw data – the reports themselves.

A powerful reason why scientists have not taken a serious look at the data over the past several years is the prevalence of many misconceptions about the nature of UFO reports and of the people who make them. I speak here only of the puzzling reports; there is little point to concern ourselves with reports that can be easily traced to balloons, satellites, meteors, etc. Neither is there any point to take account of vague, oral or written reports which contain few information bits. We need only be concerned with "hard data," defined here as reports made by several responsible witnesses, of sightings which lasted a reasonable length of time, and which were reported in a coherent manner.

I have, especially of late, strongly urged the Air Force, in my capacity as scientific consultant, to seek the aid of physical and social scientists of stature in making a respectable, scholarly study of the UFO phenomenon. It is my considered opinion that selected UFO reports deserve at least as much attention as a Brink's robbery, a kidnapping, a counterfeiting ring or a narcotics case. An investigative process in depth, with follow-through, is necessary here if, after 20 years of confusion, we want some answers.

Now that the first firm steps have been taken toward such a study, I believe I can be of some service to my colleagues in various fields by setting forth something of what I have learned during my "travels," particularly as it relates to frequently made statements about UFOs which may lead to misconceptions they may unwittingly subscribe to. Some of these statements are:

(1) Only UFO "buffs" report UFOs: The exact opposite is much nearer the truth. Only a negligible handful of reports submitted to the Air Force, or to any other organization so far as I know, are from the "true believers," the same who attend UFO conventions and who are members of the "gee-whiz" groups. These people, closely akin to cultists, are so certain in their own minds that the earth is being patrolled by outside, higher and always benign intelligences (who give repeated warnings to homo sapiens – often delivered by mental telepathy – to ban the bomb and in general, to behave) that they have no need for evidence. Why gather data? Who needs evidence? It has been my experience that quite generally the truly puzzling reports come from people who have not given much or any thought to UFOs, generally considering them "bunk" until shaken by their own experience.

(2) UFOs are reported by unreliable, unstable, and uneducated people: This is, of course, true. But UFOs are reported in even greater numbers by reliable, stable, and educated people. The better, more articulate and coherent reports predicate a fairly high threshold of intelligence; dullards rarely overcome the inertia inherent in getting down to making a written report.

(3) UFOs are never reported by scientifically trained people: This is unequivocally false. Some of the very best, most coherent reports have come from scientifically trained people. It is true, however, that scientists are among the most reluctant to make a report, and to have it made public. I have been the recipient of several such reports where the witnesses felt they should report, from a sense of duty, but did not wish to submit a public report. Reports from the scientifically trained are usually accompanied by disclaimers to the effect that they "don't believe in flying saucers" but that nonetheless they have seen something which they cannot decipher. The letters or reports sent to me generally end on a note of plaintive wonderment; they sincerely wish to know what it was they saw. Anonymity is generally requested; the request is honored.

(4) UFOs never are seen clearly or at close range but are seen under conditions of great uncertainty and always reported vaguely: By definition, when we speak of the body of puzzling reports that have accumulated through the years we exclude all those which the above description fits. By this definition, a "puzzling" report is one which leaves only two alternatives: the witness is psychotic or a congenital liar, or the witness clearly saw something that we, at least, cannot readily explain. Good physical explanations may exist – indeed, must exist, in a rational world – and this is precisely the reason I called for scientific attention to the UFO phenomenon. It is such reports, and only such reports, that I have felt deserved the attention of physical and social scientists of stature with a respectable and scholarly study. I have in my files several hundred reports which are real brain teasers and could easily be made the subject of profitable discussion among physical and social scientists alike.

(5) The Air Force has no evidence that UFOs are extraterrestrial or represent advanced technology of any kind: This is a true statement, and an honest one, but which is widely interpreted to mean that there is evidence against the two hypotheses. The unidentified cases remain unidentified and hence cannot be used in answering this question. The misinterpretations of conventional objects, etc., do not enter here. As long as there are "unidentifieds" the question must obviously remain open. If we knew what they were, they would no longer be UFOs – they would be IFOs, Identified Flying Objects! And then, of course, there would be no point to this letter. If you know the answer beforehand, it isn't research.

No truly scientific investigation of the UFO phenomenon ever has been undertaken, despite the great volume of "hard data." May we not indeed be making the same mistake the French Academy of Sciences made when they dismissed, out of hand, stories of "stones that fell from the sky." (How gullible can people get – a stone falling from the sky, indeed!) Finally, however, meteorites were made respectable in the eyes of science.

(6) UFO reports are generated by publicity: Positive feedback is undoubtedly at work when sightings are widely publicized. We shall always have the "me too" contingent with us. On the other hand, some of the sightings that are reported at times of high publicity come from reliable people who request anonymity, and who state that if they had not heard of reports from other ostensibly reliable persons, they would never have mentioned their own experience for fear of ridicule. One cannot deny that there is stimulated emission of UFO reports, but it is unwarranted to assert that this is the sole cause of high incidence of UFO reports.

(7) UFOs have never been sighted on radar or photographed by meteor or satellite tracking cameras: This statement is not equivalent to saying that radars, meteor cameras and satellite tracking stations have not picked up "oddities" on their scopes or films that have remained unidentified. It has been lightly assumed that although unidentified, the oddities were not unidentifiable as conventional objects. One should consider, however, the existence of such odd photographs as those of a "retrograde satellite," taken in 1958, and the puzzling reports from several Moonwatch teams during the IGY [International Geophysical Year, 1957-58]. I have seen photographs taken with the Baker-Nunn tracking cameras that contained unexplained "satellite" trails; at that time optical satellite tracking was my responsibility but there was little that could be done about these oddities. Very possibly they were trails of balloons or unusual aircraft, but they never have been positively identified.

Thus, the UFO situation rests. My concern stems not from hearing a few reports selected for their sensational aspects, but from noting a pattern emerge after many years of "monitoring" the phenomenon. This pattern suggests that "something is going on." What pattern? The "hard data" cases contain frequent allusions to recurrent kinematic, geometric and luminescent characteristics. The combination of "hovering," "wobbling" and "rapid takeoff" is an example of the first;

the oval shapes in both the "large" and "small" varieties, are an example of the second; and the flashing lights and ofttimes brilliant lights whose glare is uncomfortable, are an example of the third.

I cannot dismiss the UFO phenomenon with a shrug. I have begun to feel that there is a tendency in 20th century science to forget that there will be a 21st century science, and indeed, a 30th century science, from which vantage points our knowledge of the universe may appear quite different than it does to us. We suffer, perhaps, from temporal provincialism, a form of arrogance that has always irritated posterity.

Sincerely yours,<br>
J. Allen Hynek<br>
Dearborn Observatory<br>
Northwestern University

# Why Science Should Investigate the Evidence for ET Visitation

## Rosemary Ellen Guiley

Item: More than 100 exoplanets have been discovered in our own part of the galaxy in recent years, raising the likelihood of extraterrestrial life in our neighborhood.

Item: If ET life exists, at least some of them – the more technologically advanced – have the capability of visiting Earth in accordance with modern physics, via parallel universes, wormholes and warp drives that are faster than the speed of light. Or, they may have far more advanced means of travel than we can identify at present.

Item: A substantial body of high-quality eyewitness reports of UFOs and ETs has accumulated since 1947, indicating that we are indeed being visited by extraterrestrial beings.

Question: So, where *are* they?

That question, known as "Fermi's paradox," has had no adequate answer for more than 50 years. Four respected physicists say it's now time for a serious scientific reexamination of the presence of ETs. Old arguments dismissing the possibility of ET visitations no longer hold their water.

Drs. James Deardorff, Bernard Haisch, Bruce Maccabee and Hal E. Puthoff are co-authors of "Inflation-Theory Implications for Extraterrestrial Visitation," published in the *Journal of the British Interplanetary Society* in 2005. The scientists say that "open scientific research" on the Extraterrestrial Hypothesis (ETH) is needed, with special attention paid to high-quality UFO reports from eyewitnesses.

Fermi's paradox originated in 1950. One day over lunch in Los Alamos, Enrico Fermi posed the "Where are they?" question to colleagues. The question is still being asked more than 50 years later. Science has been dismissive of the ETH, thanks in part to the lack of conclusive hard evidence and the routine discrediting of eyewitness reports.

The authors of the *JBIS* article note that discoveries by Australian astronomers of the number of sun-like stars in Earth's vicinity point to the likelihood of a significant habitable zone in our Milky Way. Furthermore, the Earth is comparatively young. Thus, civilizations on older planets probably would have found us by now.

In Fermi's day, arguments against visitation were based on estimations of space travel at 5 to 10 percent of the speed of light. The galactic distances are so vast that ET arrivals here would be unlikely, according to proponents of the "we are alone" theory.

But current physics and astrophysics theories posit that visitation may not be so unlikely after all. Wormholes or "cosmic subways" could create shortcuts through space-time. Faster than light travel is part of inflation theory – the Big Bang – and could contract space-time. And, ETs might exist in parallel dimensions or universes, where speed of light might be different than in our universe.

The authors of the paper devote considerable attention to the history of eyewitness sightings and close encounters since 1947. (However, most of the references to specific UFO cases were deleted by the journal editor, except for articles Maccabee had published in the scientific literature more than two decades ago.) Of significance is the Condon Report in 1968, directed by Professor Edward U. Condon, which reflected his own admitted personal bias against evidence in favor of ET visitations.

Remarkable sightings have continued into the present, and governments around the world have released information about them. Many eyewitnesses are highly credible individuals, contrary to debunking efforts that attempt to portray them as unreliable. "This ridicule factor has prevented many serious investigators from even attempting to report their findings within journals preferred by most scientists," the authors say.

While eyewitness events convince some individuals and UFO analysts, the authors say that there has been no sustained event of sufficient magnitude to convince the world media or many scientists. However, the authors say, "We suspect that this chary behavior may be no accident."

The authors consider hypotheses that have been put forward to explain why ET visitors may prefer contained or covert contact. Called the zoo, nursery, embargo and quarantine hypotheses, these arguments posit that Earth may be under observation (zoo); may be too young to handle the explosive effects of contact (nursery); or may be off-limits according to galactic codes or laws (embargo and quarantine).

## Cheers – or jeers?

Asking scientists to take ET visitation seriously is no small matter, however. As anyone interested in ufology well knows, it's a topic relegated to the fringes of the fringe. Will this article placed in a peer-reviewed scientific journal make a difference? The answer may well be yes, judging from the initial responses the authors have received.

Three of the authors – Deardorff, Puthoff and Maccabee – gave FATE some post-publication feedback:

**Guiley: Why is your article important to scientists and ufologists?**

**Deardorff:** We hope that it will give them motivation to try to get their own analyses into publications that mainstream science reads and is comfortable with. It might be, however, that some scientists who are stuck on the "We are the Crown of Creation" syndrome will instead try to denigrate *JBIS* – the messenger journal in this case – to a non-scientific status as a result of our article therein.

**Puthoff:** One of the issues faced by scientists with regard to consideration of ET visitation is the taboo nature of the subject, at least with regard to the possibility that some UFO sightings might be a signature of such visitation. Therefore, the publication of our article in a well-respected scientific journal makes it a little safer for others to follow up with serious scientific investigation of their own. The "ridicule curtain" has been breached to some extent.

**Maccabee:** Previous articles have generally argued that UFO sighting reports are either misidentifications, mental aberrations or hoaxes. So far as we know, this is the first article in a refereed, mainstream journal to propose that UFO sightings be studied to find out if any of them are evidence of ET visitation.

**Guiley: What response have you gotten from both camps – science and ufology?**

**Deardorff:** Just the expected polarized opinions. Fortunately, the favorable responses have outnumbered the angry, derisive responses.

**Puthoff:** The responses from scientists, and from the scientific press, have been quite positive. Publication of the article has been treated in a very straightforward and informative manner. Requests for interviews came in from all over the globe, and several serious stories were written and published in the general press. Publication of the article also generated a positive response from those devoting their efforts to investigating UFO reports, as it brought some well-deserved legitimacy to their efforts to see scientists take the subject seriously.

**Maccabee:** Some congratulations from ufologists on having a paper published and faint criticism by open-minded skeptics. No direct attempt at debunking – yet. I expect it, however, eventually.

**Guiley: How can serious scientific inquiry on the Extraterrestrial Hypothesis (ETH) be initiated?**

**Deardorff:** By breaking the hold on the "ridicule factor," which our paper attempts to do in its own small way.

**Puthoff:** First of all, the SETI (Search for Extraterrestrial Intelligence) community has gained scientific credibility over the past few decades, given that the search for electromagnetic or other signals from hypothesized ET civilizations is now generally regarded by the scientific community as a serious scientific enterprise. In addition, another step in the right direction was seen in the commissioning of the Rockefeller-funded Sturrock Panel which brought together scientists to examine claimed UFO data in an impassioned way. This resulted in publication of the book *UFO Enigma*.

Also, a number of other countries, such as France, have initiated serious government investigation of UFO sightings by their gendarmerie, with the results being made available to the public in the form of detailed reports. And of course, the ongoing NASA effort to investigate the possibility of life on other planets constitutes yet another effort in this direction. As a result, explorations of the possibility of ETH-related scientific issues are already underway.

**Maccabee:** Serious inquiry already goes on, and some of it is even scientific, albeit at a very low level of support – ufologists fund their own investigations.

## Funds and facts

Scientific research requires funds and data. Obtaining money for serious research in ufology is an ongoing issue. One significant source of grant money came from Laurance S. Rockefeller, who in 1996 approached physicist Peter A. Sturrock, president of the Society for Scientific Exploration (SSE), about examining the UFO evidence. The result was the Sturrock Panel referenced by Puthoff above, which included nine scientists, and was headed by Sturrock.

The panel was the first independent review of UFO phenomena in more than 30 years. In 1997 the panel held an informal workshop with UFO investigators to examine physical evidence. In 1998, the panel released its findings that the physical evidence linked to some sightings warranted more scientific study. *UFO Enigma: A New Review of the Physical Evidence,* Sturrock's report and analysis of the panel's work, was published in 1999.

If enough scientific interest in UFOs builds, will other major sources of funding become available?

A continuing stream of data depends on experiencers who report sightings and contact. Thus, experiencers need also to overcome the "ridicule factor" and be willing to report encounters and sightings.

*Rosemary Ellen Guiley: Author and researcher in the paranormal, UFO and cryptid fields, and Executive Editor of* FATE.

FATE April 2005

# An Interview with Dr. Jacques Vallee
## George W. Earley

*[Footnoted, followed by a response from Jerome Clark.]*
In 1980, Jacques Vallee "disappeared" from organized ufology. The author of several groundbreaking (and often controversial) UFO books, a onetime associate of (and coauthor with) the late Dr. J. Allen Hynek, he vanished almost as quickly and quietly as a UFO itself. Almost a decade would pass before Vallee reappeared; when he did, he aroused even more controversy than he had in the 1970s.

Vallee's reappearance was signaled by publication of two books. *Dimensions* (1989) sought to show that the phenomenon we call UFOs has been with humanity throughout – and likely even before – recorded history. His second book, *Confrontations* (1990), chastised ufologists as scientifically inept investigators, detailed the in-depth and hands-on investigations (many of them done outside the US) he undertook during the 1980s, and expressed his strong belief that UFOs and their allegedly attendant beings were likely not extraterrestrial, but interdimensional forms.

I caught up with him in Portland, Oregon [in 1991], and between his early morning appearance on a local TV show and a press conference, the following tape-recorded conversation ensued.

**Earley:** I saw the program on TV this morning and you mentioned the Costa Rica [UFO] photograph. I looked at the one in *Confrontations* and the analysis of it and it still seems inconclusive. What do you feel we need to have for a photo to be thoroughly acceptable not only to the scientific community but also to the media and the public?

**Vallee:** Well, in this case we are taking the analysis step by step. We are purposely very careful, not making any claims that we can't prove as we go along.

The first thing that was done was to work from a second generation negative that I brought back from Costa Rica. Dick Haines (1) and I published an initial article in the *Journal of Scientific Exploration*. (2) When that article was refereed and reviewed, a couple of referees raised questions about what the image could be and what artifacts could have caused it. Now we have the original negative which I have succeeded in getting out of Costa Rica. It is a photograph taken by a mapping aircraft of the government of Costa Rica and it belongs to the government. What I have now is the original uncut negative, the frame that shows the object, the frame before and the frame after, taken at 20 second intervals. We have looked at it, magnified it, printed it with different densities, and so on. That eliminates all the claims of possible artifacts. We know this is not a double exposure, we know this is not a fine particle trapped in the film ... this is a real image. It is a large image. The next step is to digitize it. We do not have access to such a place here [in America] but I know people in France who can do it, with superb facilities for computer photo analysis. We are waiting for them to digitize the frames and to do enhancement and comparisons of one frame to the next.

**Earley:** I'll be interested in hearing the results of their work. Now, during your TV appearance today, just before and after each commercial break, the station used some of those controversial saucer photos taken in Switzerland by Edward Meier. Has anyone analyzed them? I know there have been a couple of books about him, but I don't believe his claims have ever been seriously examined.

**Vallee:** In the case of Meier, the negatives have never been available, to my knowledge. Without the negatives, one can do nothing. So, it goes back to a question of belief. I am very, very skeptical of the Meier case. I've been to his place in Switzerland. Nobody can tell me this is an average Swiss farmer ... [chuckles] ... the man has led an extremely interesting life. The photographs themselves are not convincing. No one will be able to tell for sure until we can work from the negatives and the negatives have never been available. And there's no good reason for withholding them. In a situation where someone has had a genuine experience, there should be full disclosure. There is no reason to hide anything.

**Earley:** I agree. I would also note that the space beings he says he's meeting with are more like those described by George Adamski in the 1950s than the beings that are reported today. I don't know how you feel about this, but it raises a warning flag for me.

**Vallee:** Yes. And the place ... I was there last summer [1989]. The place is run like a cult. Visitors are screened by members of his group. He is not at all living in poverty, getting up at sunup to work in the fields. He has a large house, with the flag of his organization in front of it, a guest book which has been signed by every TV station in Japan which has come through there. There is a satellite antenna to pick up foreign television broadcasts ... this is an organized cult. It is not just the average farmer who has happened to see UFOs.

## Gulf Breeze

**Earley:** Very interesting. Have you talked with Dr. Bruce Maccabee about the Gulf Breeze case?

**Vallee:** Yes, I have. I respect Dr. Maccabee, he's a good scientist. I've looked at the photographs, spent two to three hours with him in Washington. I should qualify this – I don't like to talk about cases I have not investigated myself. I have not gone to Gulf Breeze purposely, I am not trying to investigate it. As you know from my book, I put the highest priority on cases that have not been reported and cases that are not big media cases with fanfare ... those are the cases where I can achieve something within my limitations, where I can get somewhere. I like the cases that have been very quiet or where interest has disappeared over the years. Then I can go to the site and meet the people and be seriously involved. This is certainly not the case in Gulf Breeze.

Now on the technical questions I have about Gulf Breeze, I've never gotten an answer.

One question is: What is the source of the illumination of these objects? It is a fairly straightforward technical question.

Another question is: Why don't we have a spectrum of the illumination? The object appeared again and again and again; it appeared often enough that the witness could be supplied with a camera that had four different lenses on it. Well, it would be a simple thing to sacrifice one of the lenses and put a [diffraction] grating in front of the objective [lens] and get a spectrum and then we would know once and for all if it's a good old 200-watt Sylvania light bulb in there or if it is something unknown to physics. At least we would know that. From the photographs you can't tell.

Another thing that is very, very disturbing is that, as you know, the witness, Ed Walters, has a record. Well, that is neither here nor there – people with records see UFOs just like people with no records. But that does have an influence on the way one would analyze a sighting. The fact that he has a record is not disclosed in the book. I think that's wrong! I feel there should be full disclosure.

**Earley:** There was a vague mention of an "indiscretion" or something like that. I would note that in a recent issue of Jim Moseley's *Saucer Smear* newsletter (3), Walters writes that because of "my reputation as a responsible business man and community leader" he has been granted "a Full Pardon" by Florida Governor Bob Martinez. Of course, that doesn't take away the guilt of what he did ... I know Phil Klass loves to get into things like that. He pointed out that Travis Walton had also been charged with forgery.

**Vallee:** I think that's relevant and it should always be disclosed. There should be no question in disclosing it. The fact that in this case there is no full disclosure, that the book presented him as a pillar of the community, I find that wrong.

**Earley:** I think the pardon came after the book was published. Perhaps it will be put in the second edition.

I'd like to talk about witness harassment and ridicule. You mentioned this topic in your book; I believe in one instance you wrote of "vandalism." Was this to a victim's home or car?

**Vallee:** If you remember, there were several cases like this. There was a policeman in the Midwest, Herbert Schirmer, who suffered from harassment. Even in the case of Lonnie Zamorra, he was harassed and had to leave the police department. The kids, when he tried to arrest them in Socorro [New Mexico], would say, "Why are you after me? Look at that flying saucer over there. It's going faster than I am. Why don't you arrest it and leave me alone?" In the famous case in Michigan, the "swamp gas" case, the witness's house was pelted with beer bottles and Coke bottles and cans ... just the reaction of the friendly local community.

**Earley:** The police chief, in Alabama I think it was, who took the picture of an alleged entity ... Greenhaw, was it? I think he resigned because of the hassles he had. Have any of your fellow scientists done any sociological studies as to why there should be this reaction to UFO reports?

**Vallee:** Not any formal studies. It is a normal human reaction in a way; there is a reaction of laughter to relieve tension and the fear of the unknown. It's nice to be able to laugh at it and it makes you look smart. It is a normal reaction by people who don't want to be bothered by such things. I don't know what it will take for people to grow up and recognize this phenomenon as something very important. I hope that my book will be a contribution in that direction. Among my colleagues it has started to have that effect. After reading the book they understand that this is obviously not just a bunch of uneducated people in the countryside sitting by the river and watching flying saucers come by.

**Earley:** So, you're getting as positive reaction from your colleagues in the United States as well as in France?

**Vallee:** Absolutely.

## Cosmic implications

**Earley:** That's encouraging, because what it gets down to is how do we develop a proof that will allow people to take this seriously? Why are people ignoring the, shall we say, "cosmic" implications of the UFO phenomenon?

**Vallee:** The people who are interested in the UFO phenomenon ... we've been guilty of pushing the extraterrestrial theory to the exclusion of everything else. The word from many people in the public and in the scientific community is either UFOs don't exist, and it is all illusions and mistakes and hoaxes and so forth, or we are being visited by beings from outer space. It seems to be either one or the other.

Well, it doesn't have to be one or the other. What I find is that people start paying attention when you tell them, "Hey, of course it could be aliens or a form of intelligence from outer space, but it could be other things too!" Then they want to know more, they start thinking. Before they had to decide between not believing the witnesses or agreeing that we were being visited by aliens. People have reacted negatively to that narrow choice. Scientists have certainly reacted negatively to it. They say, "Oh yeah? If they are space aliens, how and why do they come here?" I had that reaction yesterday at a radio station in Seattle. "Why do they do these absurd things people say they do? Why do they look like us?"

We have to deal with the fact that while this phenomenon is very complex, it does not have to be extraterrestrial necessarily. That opens up many other hypotheses including interdimensionality, which is now mainstream physics. There are theories about the universe having more than four dimensions, and to me the UFO phenomenon is interesting to the extent that it is forcing us to ask those questions and to test some of those new and exciting theories. When you say that, scientists become interested once again because it means that the UFO problem is not a closed system anymore.

What has surprised me is that when you start proposing such ideas, the people who react the most negatively, not to say venomously, are not the skeptics but the people in the UFO community themselves. I have been astonished by this violent reaction and you may have seen the comments of Budd Hopkins and of Jerry Clark (4) calling me a flake for opening up these possibilities.

I've argued before, as you know, with Donald Menzel and I've argued with Philip Klass, yet I've never experienced such polemics. Mind you, I don't mind the polemics. I'm not particularly looking for it, but if it happens, it happens. Yet I've never encountered the kind of vitriolic reaction as I have with Jerry Clark, which was totally uncalled for. It just came out of nowhere as far as I'm concerned. That taught me an important lesson, though, that I'd not realized before: parochialism within the UFO community itself may be what is preventing us from being heard by the scientific world.

**Earley:** I think that could be a possibility. The "house divided" effect.

**Vallee:** Jerome Clark is reacting almost as if I had questioned something very sacred for him, something that must not be questioned by someone who calls himself a UFO researcher. I'm questioning the dogma that these beings are ETs. Yet when I listen to the witnesses, which is what I try to do carefully, they tell me they see objects appearing out of nowhere and disappearing on the spot. They don't necessarily see things that take off and go up in the sky and go through the atmosphere. In some cases they do, but in many cases they describe objects that seem to have the ability to operate on space-time, to manipulate space-time. If there is a form of consciousness that does that, if there is a technology that does that, then it opens up all kinds of questions that we have never really considered seriously. From a scientific point of view, number one, it makes a lot more sense. Number two, it is much richer in terms of what we can do with it in our own research.

**Earley:** It is, of course, a regrettable fact that the scientific community, by and large, has rejected the UFO phenomenon out of hand without making any real study of it. I've talked to Isaac Asimov. He speaks of "UFO maniacs" in a recent book (5) on the NASA SETI program, yet he knows nothing of UFOs. When you try to pin him down about his skepticism, he says: "Well, I've devoted enough of my time to this and I have many other things to do." Carl Sagan does the same thing. A very personable man but very shallow some respects, particularly in regard to the UFO phenomenon.

**Vallee:** They've never taken time to study the cases themselves. All they know about it is what they read in the *National Enquirer*.

**Earley:** Are you saying that to a large degree you wrote *Confrontations* for the scientific community, and that while you are hoping it will have an impact on the public at large, basically you were speaking to your colleagues?

**Vallee:** I'm trying to show that, number one, the data is robust enough that it can be studied scientifically. There is no lack of parameters that are quantifiable, there is no lack of data from technically trained observers. Number two, I am showing that the phenomenon also has important medical and physiological implications that should be studied. A lot of attention has recently been placed – and rightly so – on the abduction phenomenon. That is fine, but beyond the abduction phenomenon there are other types of impacts that should be documented and studied, [such as] the medical and physiological impact. I'm trying to call attention to that.

### Abductions and hypnosis

**Earley:** You mentioned Hopkins' disagreement with your theory as to the possible origin of the aliens. Do you still feel the abduction phenomenon is a real one?

**Vallee:** I've never said otherwise. People have tried to imply that I was rejecting the abduction phenomenon and I never have. As you know, both in *Confrontations* and in *Dimensions,* I even talk about abduction cases I've studied. In *Confrontations* you will find the case of the woman I call "Mrs. Victor" and several other cases.

In Happy Camp, California, for example, there was an abduction case, among many other things. In some cases, I have studied those incidents with the help of hypnotists. But I surely would not do the hypnosis myself as some abductionists do. As I have said before, and I will say it at every occasion, this is unethical and unscientific. What they [the abduction hypnotists] are getting is not the truth. They are wrongly assuming that they are looking at the first-level interpretations of what the witnesses have encountered. In many of those hypnosis sessions you will find that leading questions are being used. Besides, there is obvious screening or self-selection on the part of the people who come forward to be hypnotized. There is a framework that is put on the experience itself.

The tragedy is that once that kind of framework has been put on the experience, you cannot go back. I've had a number of people who have been studied and hypnotized, people who have been mentioned in some of the more prominent books on abduction, who have come to me saying, "My experience was much wider than what is described in the book. The author took things out of context to fit them into his preconceived framework, to put them in his book, but I need help to deal with other aspects of my experience that nobody wanted to look at."

I'm not in a position to help these people because they've already been hypnotized a number of times, and they are stuck in a certain framework. I don't know of any way one can go back and re-hypnotize these people to get back to the original experience. Which is why in many cases a psychiatrist using hypnosis in his work will tell you that you have to be very careful, and that in many cases hypnosis is not even the proper form of investigation.

**Earley:** That's why I was frankly appalled at Dr. Edith Fiore's book (6) because she "learned" hypnosis over one weekend and then began using it the following Monday. And now she thinks she is an abductee after having been hypnotized by Dr. James Harder. I understand Rima Laibow is saying she's an abductee. It seems to me there is a lot of self-contamination and pollution in this business.

But let's take a scenario here. Suppose I came to you and said I've been having disturbing dreams and I've read things in newspapers and magazines about abductions; maybe I've been abducted; you're the first person I've come to about this. What would your step-by-step procedure be with a person who approached you in that manner?

**Vallee:** I think witnesses should only go to trained people. Hypnosis is a complex and dangerous thing; people should only go to clinical psychologists or MDs for that kind of work. There is an objection to that, which I have heard from Jerome Clark and other people in the UFO field, saying that many witnesses don't have access to such experts. So, Budd Hopkins and Dave Jacobs and others are performing a valuable service when they do it themselves because the medical professionals are not always available to do it.

Well, it's obviously a flawed argument. It's like you're coming to me and saying, "I need a triple [heart] bypass. Would you please take your kitchen knife and do it because my doctor doesn't want to do it?" I'm not qualified to do a triple bypass and I'm not qualified to hypnotize anybody and I'm not going to learn the technique so I can start hypnotizing people left and right. Again, I think this is unethical and unscientific and it doesn't get us to the kind of UFO data we need.

In the cases when this situation has happened, what I've done is to go to professionals I know. I would not discuss the case with a witness. I would say, "Look, we are going to get to know each other. You are going to tell me about yourself, but let's not talk about UFOs. Please don't read any more on the subject for a few weeks until we can get you to see someone who is trained in hypnosis."

In one case I went to a friend of mine who is a clinical psychologist and he said, "You won't need hypnosis with this person, there are other ways, there are much more sophisticated techniques that can be used to help people remember what happened to them, under their own control."

In certain cases, a "day dreaming" type of technique can help the person remember things at his or her own pace. This could also come through dreams, it could come through drawings, it could take a long time, like months. But this is much less intrusive than saying, "You-Are-Now-Under-My-Power-and-You-Will-Remember-the-Time-When-the-Aliens-Took-You," which is very often what you hear on those ridiculous abduction tapes.

**Earley:** This goes along with a recent book review (7) that examined hypnosis and questioned if hypnosis per se actually existed, or whether we can, by simply relaxing people, enable them to be in a fully waking state but simply have more access to their memories.

**Vallee:** Again, I'm not a specialist of that field and I'm just relaying what different professionals have told me. They disagree among themselves, so I should qualify that. There are obviously some instances where hypnosis is the technique of choice. There is another case in my files in which I went to a psychiatrist who is trained in hypnosis. He told me he did not want to do it. His reasons showed the reaction of a true professional. He said, "I should not be the one doing it for two reasons. First of all, I do not have enough recent clinical experience with hypnosis. And second, I know you. I've read your books and you're a friend of mine and I know too much about the subject. We should find somebody who is qualified, who knows hypnosis, who has an open mind on UFOs but does not have a personal framework." It is difficult, but such people exist.

Let me mention another case I've worked on recently, the case of a man with a Silicon Valley computer company, who came to me because he remembered seeing some objects over Hawaii. He wanted to be hypnotized because he felt there had been some action of that type [abduction]. I took him to a team of two doctors. One is not a psychiatrist but an MD who uses hypnosis in his medical practice, and the other one is a psychologist who teaches hypnosis to psychologists. In other words, he is doing research on hypnosis and he teaches it.

I asked them what kind of methodology could be used in abduction cases and how would they go about it. They said the only way we should do it is to use the standards of admissibility of hypnosis in court. The state of California has published some very strict guidelines for when hypnosis is admissible in the courts of that state. These guidelines are perfect. They are tailor-made for us in UFO research. Hypnosis is not admissible unless everything is on video tape including the induction phase, so you can see if there are leading questions, you can check if there is full disclosure in the beginning by the hypnotist on what the person is to expect, and so on. You should also have physiological measurements; for example, skin response measurements and pulse measurements. You never see this in UFO abduction research.

In this case, the two doctors set up a number of instruments that were visible to the cameras. There were two cameras shooting at the same time, so you could always see the instruments as you heard the answers; you could have chronological correlation. Another expert could later say, "That person, doctor, was not hypnotized when he said this. He was not in a state of hypnosis." Different experts could challenge the data and argue. Otherwise what you have is pure garbage, you just have someone saying something on tape.

In the case of this man, we found that indeed he remembered a lot about the incident in Hawaii but that the real incident did not happen in Hawaii. It was many years before and there may have been an abduction in the south of the United States when he was in a car with his parents. At that point he became so agitated that the two doctors got him out of hypnosis, which is precisely the point where a ufologist would have jumped up and down and said, "Oh goody, let's find out what happened! Did they have big eyes, were they grey, which planet did they take you to," and so on.

But the doctors stopped everything and said, "We are not going to do anything further until we have a therapy contract with this man. Obviously, this is an extremely traumatic experience for him and if we pick it up again we will pick it up as a part of a course of therapy." That is the reaction of true professionals in the business, where you have to worry about possibly causing harm to the patient and keeping your license and malpractice and everything else – all the things ufologists treat very lightly.

**Earley:** Have they gone deeper into it?

**Vallee:** We did not pursue it yet. It will be up to him [the subject] to decide if he wants to do more.

### Animal mutilations
**Earley:** You wrote some introductory remarks to Linda Moulton Howe's book, *An Alien Harvest*.

**Vallee:** There are certain parts of the book I would not condone or agree with, but it is her right to publish it, and I wanted to support her work on mutilations. I think she is raising a number of important questions the UFO community has been ignoring.

**Earley:** Do you feel that the mutilations are not being done by a normal human agency?

**Vallee:** Ahhh, let me put it this way. I made it clear in *Confrontations* that I was not going to discuss mutilations even though they were a possibly relevant subject. I've done a number of field studies of mutilation cases on the same level as this in which there was certainly no classic explanation for what had happened to the animals. The witnesses had seen objects in the sky at about the same time the mutilations had happened. That doesn't mean that I can prove a correlation and that's where I stop. I do have an open mind on that. Linda is doing some very good work in that field. More people should be looking at it. I cannot tell you that there is a link between UFOs and mutilations.

**Earley:** Would you be planning to publish your research at some point?

**Vallee:** I don't know. I might.

**Earley:** Thank you very much for your time, Dr. Vallee. I am sure FATE readers will be interested in your remarks.

Notes:
1) Dr. Richard Haines, a retired senior scientist formerly employed by NASA, is the author of several books on UFOs including *Advanced Aerial Devices Reported During the Korean War,* ILDA Press, 1990.
2) "Photo Analysis of an Aerial Disc Over Costa Rica" by Richard F. Haines & Jacques Vallee, *Journal of Scientific Exploration,* Vol 3, No. 2, 1989. A response by Haines & Vallee, based on an examination of the original negative, to referee questions, appeared in Vol 4, No. 1, 1990 as "Photo Analysis of an Aerial Disc Over Costa Rica: New Evidence."
3) *Saucer Smear* Vol. 37 No. 3, April 30, 1990.
4) "The Thickets of Magonia" by Jerome Clark, *International UFO Reporter,* Jan-Feb. 1990.
5) *First Contact,* ed. by Ben Bova & Byron Preiss, NAL, 1990.
6) *Encounters* by Edith Fiore, PhD, Doubleday,1989.
7) "Demystifying Hypnosis," *Skeptical Inquirer,* Vol. 14, No. 3/Spring 1990. The book under review is *Hypnosis: The Cognitive-Behavioral Perspective* edited by Nicholas P. Spanos & John F. Chaves, Prometheus Books, 1989. Also see *They Call It Hypnosis* by Robert A. Baker, Prometheus Books; 1990, pages 23-25.

## Jerome Clark Responds to Jacques Vallee

Because Jacques Vallee mentions me – unfavorably in each instance – several times in this interview, I have been given the opportunity to comment.

Vallee's animosity toward me stems from a long, *partially* critical review of his *Confrontations* (1990) I wrote for *International UFO Reporter (IUR),* which I edit for the J. Allen Hynek Center for UFO Studies. [See issue January-February 1990.] Vallee complains that the review was "venomous." In that review I characterized his book as "one of the most interesting...you are likely ever to read...Vallee has significantly broadened our knowledge of the UFO phenomenon...a work of enduring value." I wrote that Vallee emerges as "something of a hero...decent, open-minded and compassionate...(Y)ou will find [*Confrontations*] a fascinating and exciting book." If that's venom, give me a *big* bite.

In view of what *Confrontations* has to say about ufologists – not the credophiles and nut cases, mind you, but the most serious and thoughtful of them – these remarks were pretty generous, though I was certainly sincere in expressing them despite my misgivings about portions of the book, which I urge you, by the way, to run out and purchase. Be sure, however, to take a salt shaker with you.

I wrote Vallee (whom I have known and liked for many years) more than once to tell him that the pages of *IUR* were open to any response to my critique – I hoped for a detailed, to-the-point one – that he cared to write.

My major problem with his book, aside from the inadequacies of its analysis and the author's seeming ignorance of much of current ufology, was my sense that in not interacting with fellow ufologists (and his book depicts them as, yes, flakes – his depiction of virtually all ufologists other than himself is not significantly different from CSICOP's), Vallee had removed himself from a critical community – those friends and associates to whom any professional must answer. I felt that if Vallee had been willing to discuss his theories with informed, intelligent colleagues before rushing into print, he would have written a better book.

My review, I feel, was kinder to Vallee than he was to the rest of us. Vallee has refused every offer to discuss the substance of my criticisms, which were not *ad hominem,* but substantive and had nothing to do, as Vallee would have it, with a defense of the sacred or theological – which seems to be the argument those on losing ends of debates in these areas ultimately always resort to: see, for example, Paul Kurtz's hilariously uninformed treatment of ufology in *The Transcendental Temptation: A Critique of Religion and the Paranormal* (1986). Nonetheless, I can't resist observing that a leading scholarly authority on religious movement, J. Gordon Melton, has written that Vallee's views have a "paranoid" element and are based not on science but on a "religious-metaphysical approach" which has little appeal to ufologists seeking scientific validation for the UFO phenomenon. In short, perhaps Vallee should examine his own attitudes.

My problems with Vallee's theories and logic are dealt with at length in the above-mentioned *IUR* article and on pages 173-177 of my recently published book, *UFOs in the 1980s*. (There you will find, along with much else, a critique of Vallee's naïve treatment of the role of hypnosis in abduction research; you will also find that I said no such thing about hypnosis as Vallee claims I did.) So far, neither Vallee nor his many enthusiastic followers have answered a single substantive criticism, preferring to impugn my motives or engage in how-dare-you histrionics. Too bad. Ideas – and Vallee is full of ideas – (even misguided ones) deserve better.

Vallee's ignorance of current ufology is shown in his curious assertion that "we've been guilty of pushing the extraterrestrial theory to the exclusion of everything else." In fact, the extraterrestrial hypothesis has had vigorous competition in recent years from proponents of the psycho-social hypothesis and the tectonic-strain theory, both of which reject space (or extradimensional) visitors in favor of hallucinations and geophysical phenomena. Vallee's quarrel should not be with the extraterrestrial hypothesizers, who agree with him that UFOs are the product of an alien intelligence, but with those who wish to remove aliens from the UFO equation altogether.

In any case, even old-fashioned ufologists have always been willing to consider the parallel universe, other dimensional idea Vallee claims they reject. Such notions go back to the pre-1947 era, in fact, and to the occult Borderland Sciences Research Associates (formed in 1945), which has long held that UFOs are "ether ships" from other realms of reality.

Finally, I have never called Vallee a "flake," nor do I consider him one. Once, when interviewed by *Omni*, I expressed the opinion that some of Vallee's *theories* (especially those positing the existence of sinister conspiracies) are on the flaky side, and frankly it's hard for me to imagine that any intellectually sophisticated reader could disagree. But then there's probably not a person alive who doesn't harbor, even if secretly, a flaky idea or two. Yet as Professor Henry Bauer has observed, one can be wrong, even very wrong, without being irrational. As I see it, Vallee is in some ways badly mistaken, but not in any sense of the word crazy. And even when he's mistaken, he never fails to be interesting.

Vallee should not be insulted, but flattered, when his views are questioned. To be rebutted is, after all, to be taken seriously. Jacques Vallee is an entertaining, provocative presence on the UFO scene. All I'm asking, Jacques, is that you think a little harder. Is that so bad? And I promise to try to do the same.

*George W. Earley: Writer and author on UFOs.*

*Jerome Clark: Prolific author, writer and researcher on ufology and paranormal topics; FATE columnist.*

FATE July 1991

# On Remote Viewing, UFOs, and Extraterrestrials
## Ingo Swann

**A new controversy**

During the last year or so, the UFO community has found itself possessed not only by its usual problems (such as confirming that UFOs exist), but also by a new situation convulsing the community's gossip networks.

A growing number of people are claiming to use their remote viewing powers to penetrate UFOs and extraterrestrial motives, goals and civilizations. Remote viewing is apparently being thought of as a new, better psychic ability that certain Earthside individuals claim to have achieved, and advertise that with it they are achieving novel, intimate and true "viewings" (i.e., sightings) into Spaceside ET affairs.

Many long-term FATE readers probably remember the emergence in parapsychology of remote viewing in 1973-74, and FATE editors have kept abreast of its developments by publishing occasional articles. A list of references is provided at the end of this essay for those who wish to know more about the remote viewing story.

This new controversy (perhaps only a transient brouhaha) has come about because UFO investigators never before permitted mixing their work with psychic "stuff," while parapsychologists never mixed their work with UFO "stuff." And so, mixing these two "stuffs" is stirring up complaints, critical objections and worries in both communities.

This new confusion is added to the other confusing imbroglios that characterize the UFO "situation" (governmental-military cover-ups, irresponsible scientific debunking, and UFO-community leadership disputes).

I've been intimately involved in remote viewing developments for over 20 years. Many people send me alleged ET "remote viewing" reports and seek me out to ask what I think about this new situation, including the editors of FATE, who have asked me to say something about it.

### Remote viewing's key element: utilitarian value

All of our lives are shaped by discovering the utilitarian value, not only of things but also of ourselves. Remote viewing is no exception to this. And so this new brouhaha hinges on whether there is any real utilitarian value in attempting to "utilize remote viewing to penetrate UFOs and/or ETs."

But to determine the utilitarian value of something one has to be sure that one has a well-defined specimen of it in hand, and then subject it to rigorous testing that positively demonstrates any utilitarian value.

Along this line of thinking, it is worth wondering how many of those claiming to remote view ETs bothered to look up remote viewing's definition in the parapsychological literature. If they had, then they might have thought twice about claiming to be remote viewers.

I cannot, of course, control how people seek to use terms in the ways they do. Meanings shift about, and many use terms in different flip-flop ways even if clearly defined in dictionaries.

For example, take the word "sophisticated." It is derived from the Sophist philosophical school of ancient Greece. Sophists had a habit of muddling up their thinking, especially by arguments that were later proven to be fallacious. So, a sophister, as defined in the 1828 Webster's dictionary is "A disputant fallaciously subtle, an artful but insidious logician," i.e. a muddled thinker disguised as artful and logical. Most skeptics and not a few alleged psychics ultimately were proven to have been sophisters.

The 1828 Webster's dictionary defines sophisticated as to adulterate, to corrupt by something spurious or foreign, to pervert. But today the term is generally taken to mean something perfectly achieved, elegant and balanced when referring to a thing, elegant and world-wise and knowing when referring to a person. The shift in meaning came about in the 1920s when intellectuals then took pride in being artfully and elegantly insidious, and when young Hollywood needed a buzzword to describe the handsome and beautiful exteriors of their prized movie stars.

I will show ahead that anyone claiming to be a remote viewer or claiming to remote view ETs and UFOs is a sophister, one who has artfully but insidiously muddled up the established definition of remote viewing – perhaps only because they haven't bothered to look it up. A sophister – unless one important facet of their "remote viewing" is undertaken by them or ultimately provided by others.

## The origin of the term "remote viewing"

I can speak this way about the term remote viewing because it was coined, in 1971-72, by myself and Dr. Janet Mitchell, at the American Society for Psychical Research (ASPR) in New York, in association with Dr. Gertrude Schmeidler and Dr. Karlis Osis. It was coined to identify a particular kind of experiment – not a particular kind of psi ability.

There is a substantial definitional difference between coining a term to identify a type of ESP experiment and an ESP ability. It is very difficult to define a psychic ability. But it is not hard to define an experiment.

Experiments have what in science are called "protocols," more simply put as "steps" that govern how the experiment is conducted. The last step in any experimental protocol involves determining whether the experiment worked or not. Finding out if the experiment worked or not, or how well it worked, is called "confirmation," but usually more intimately spoken of as "feedback." Without feedback in some form, it cannot be known if the experiment worked. Positive feedback suggests possible utilitarian value; negative feedback, or absence of it, does not.

Different kinds of experiments need to be distinguished from one another, and so researchers settle on some easy-to-remember nomenclature or acronym that best describes what the experiment involves. Sometimes these experiment terms can be pretty silly, but even so they sometimes catch on as popular buzz words beyond the scope of identifying a particular type of experiment.

In the case of the term "remote viewing," there can be no doubt at all that it originally referred to an experimental model (never to a novel ESP ability), and there exists a voluminous and dated paper trail, the whole of which constitutes an enormous archive. A vast number of official research documents contain adequate descriptions of the original intended meaning of remote viewing. And this meaning is also found adequately displayed and demonstrated in a number of earlier popular books (see bibliography).

In late 1970, by a strange set of circumstances, I was invited by Dr. Karlis Osis and Dr. Gertrude Schmeidler to act as an experimental subject in certain ongoing experiments at the American Society of Psychical Research in New York. Dr. Osis was then the Society's research director and had taken a deep interest in out-of-body experiences (OBE) that in earlier decades had been referred to by such confusing terms as traveling clairvoyance, ecsomatic experiences, bilocation and astral projection.

Dr. Osis and colleagues were recruiting volunteers to "test" for OBE abilities via an experimental model involving a tray suspended just beneath a room's ceiling. Hanging suspended on the trays just below the ceiling, out of the subjects' sight, various objects (the targets) had been placed. The experimental goal was to ask the subjects to try to "go out of body," float up to above the trays, and then "look down and see" what was concealed on them.

The OBE experiment involved an assumption: that if the subjects correctly identified the hidden objects then they had "gone out of their bodies" in order to do so. And so, this model was called an OBE experiment.

In any event, I went to the ASPR two or three days a week for many months and tried to identify an endless series of targets – while strapped into a chair with my brain waves being monitored on an EEG machine by Janet Mitchell. At first, I was not very good at this kind of "perceiving," but as the months wore on, I got better at it.

Regardless of the ambiguous assumption, the experiments were very careful ones. A target was hidden from the subject, who was to try to perceive it. After the subject verbally reported his or her "seeing," the

*Remote viewing the hidden targets; the woman in the orange coat.*

report was compared to the object (judged) in full view of everyone, and in this way feedback was achieved as to accuracy or not.

One winter day in November 1972, I was having trouble "floating up" to the hidden targets in the windowless experimental room but happened to "notice through the walls" that a woman in a dreadful orange coat was walking down the sidewalk past the ASPR building. I first discounted this, but suddenly tore off the electrodes and got Janet Mitchell to run into the street with me to see if a woman in an orange coat was walking by the building. We tumbled down the stairs and got outside just in time to see a woman in an orange coat turning the corner.

This event was not part of the official OBE experiment, but it got me to thinking about why I should have "seen" the woman outside when the targets were inside.

Now, a subtle point needs to be made. The official experiment required that the subject "see" the specified targets. In other words, the experiment was target-focused and not "seeing" focused. If the subject did not see the targets, then the experiment was considered a failure – all of which seems sensible enough in a standard kind of way, and in fact, is the only way that feedback can be achieved for any kind of ESP test experiment, including those associated with remote viewing.

But there is a significant difference between (1) the "seeing" of the designated targets and (2) the dimensions or scope of the "seeing" itself. Yet, as I was soon to discover, all parapsychology experiments were entirely of the see-the-target only kind, and hardly any research had ever gone into the "seeing" processes and their dimensions.

It was at about this point that my see-the-target efforts, intermittently successful thereto, fell victim to the utter boredom of doing hundreds and hundreds of attempts, often 30 or more in a given afternoon. To help alleviate the boredom, I suggested that we spend a little time "playing around" with the "seeing" processes themselves. The orange-coated woman event had suggested that "seeing" might have greater "distance capabilities" than merely from the floor to the ceiling or into the next room.

Janet Mitchell and I devised a playing-around experiment in which I would try to "see" the weather conditions in distant cities. Since some kind of feedback was absolutely necessary to determine what was "seen," after my distant weather impressions had been given and recorded, Janet or someone else could immediately telephone the weather information number in the distant city and find out what the weather was doing. The cities we were to play around with "seeing" were selected by third parties. So, unless I had somehow memorized all the weather conditions in a large number of cities, it was reasonable to conclude that a "distant seeing" had taken place if the response was fed back as correct.

According to my dated and carefully preserved archives, the first long-distance "seeings" of this kind took place on the afternoon of December 8, 1971, and the first results were encouraging. But more, the processes of this kind of "seeing" were exciting and invigorating, and with this entertainment option available, my boredom alleviated, and the local target experiments resumed vigorously with results that were inexplicably better.

It was at this point that the problem of what to call the long-distance experiments emerged in order to distinguish between them and the local target experiments inside the ASPR building. We first thought of them as "traveling clairvoyance" experiments; but since this named an ability, not an experiment, I suggested that we call them "remote sensing" experiments because after all, the distant cities, such as Tucson and Denver, were remote from the ASPR in New York. Shortly, though, it became clear that I didn't just sense the sites, but experienced mental image pictures of them in a visualizing kind of way.

Without at all thinking much about it, and before the end of 1971, we began referring to the long-distance experiments as remote viewing ones, since this term seemed the most suitable. Since the psi-perceptual-processes that might account for the "seeing" were a mystery, it is again to be understood that the term remote viewing did not refer to them, or to any novel ESP ability.

From the startup of its usage, remote viewing referred to the entire experimental model, and the experiment was one only because of the feedback that could be supplied by telephoning the distant weather agency. In fact, and indeed without the feedback, one cannot tell whether any verifiable "seeing" had taken place or not, cannot tell how good or bad it was, or how efficient or inefficient it was, or whether the "viewing" was merely the result of fantasy, imagination, opinion or wishful thinking.

It was at this point (in early 1972), after thinking these matters through, that I got the three ideas (rather simple ones) that psi researchers have either missed or completely avoided:

1. Psi perceptions plus feedback = remote viewing.
2. Remote viewing minus feedback = ?

Well, remote viewing minus feedback actually equals whatever you do or do not want it to. For example, it can represent illusion to skeptics, who do not bother to study feedback even if it is available. It can represent wishful thinking to would-be psychics who do not bother to demonstrate feedback especially if it cannot be available in the first place.

These considerations led to the third rather simple idea:

3. That feedback is more important than the psi perceptions, because without it the former cannot be said either to exist or have occurred, or to what degree of accuracy. Thus, beyond any and all doubt, feedback has a great deal to do with establishing utilitarian value of psi perceptions whether they are called ESP, clairvoyance or whatever.

Feedback, then, is not trivial or incidental to the remote viewing process and protocols. It is crucial to them.

To simplify all this, we can resort to an easy-to-understand formula. Remote viewing consists of five absolutely necessary ingredients: (1) subject, (2) active ESP abilities, (3) distant target, (4) subject's recorded responses, (5) confirmatory positive feedback – all of which equals (6) the remote viewing model.

Nothing less is remote viewing.

Those alleging themselves to be remote viewers, then, cannot simply just "remote view," but are obliged also to show positive evidence of their "viewings" – e.g., positive feedback. Without the feedback, such "viewers" are merely offering unsupported accounts that may or may not be of psychic origin. Remote viewing is neither a novel psi ability, nor a convenient replacement term for psi, clairvoyance or ESP.

## Objections to muddling-up: The definition of remote viewing

I am particularly heartless regarding this matter, and for the following explicit reasons. What remote viewing does represent, in its complete protocol, was gained by two decades of untold hours of work and excruciatingly detailed research on the parts of hundreds of people, including myself.

It was gained at a cost of much money provided by hundreds of additional people who had experimental interest in ascertaining remote viewing's utilitarian value, and in identifying and understanding its psychic-dynamic processes.

Its existence as a verifiable topic for experimental research was established against hundreds of fearsome debunking attacks emanating from organized police-like sophister-skeptics bent on enforcing the scientific orthodoxy that psi is non-existent, and that claims for it are of illusory or psychopathological origin.

As a result of all these efforts, the term "remote viewing" entered the language with something akin to scientific merit, and it is this merit that a variety of individuals are now trying to colonize in attempts to imply merit for their self-styled psychic espionage attempts regarding UFOs and ETs.

If even one individual alleges himself or herself to be a remote viewer without showing how concrete positive feedback of their "viewing" can be realized, well, these people are playing into the drooling minds of sophister-skeptics just waiting to debunk not only them but also remote viewing itself, and, as well, creative ufological and parapsychological interest in its utilitarian value.

This value has yet to be proven, and it can only be proven by positive feedback. So, kids out there, where's your feedback to substantiate your "remote viewings"?

## The remote viewing-ET feedback problem

I'm not at all saying that psychic perceptions cannot be applied to the ET-UFO situation. I've openly suggested this potential data source myself. But if psychic data is derived via many people wanting to contribute it, still the hard issue of feedback is a crucial determinant regarding what to make of that data.

Some parapsychologists have referred to their work as the "Illusive Science." Well, the illusiveness of UFOs and ETs far surpasses even that terribly illusive science. So illusive, indeed, that ufologists as a group are unable to agree upon even just one UFO or ET fact – while parapsychologists as a group at least agree that psi exists.

If parapsychology is the illusive science, then clearly ufology is virtually the "Feedbackless Science" with the true exception so far of the hundreds of camcorders that have filmed UFOs. To my knowledge, UFOs and ETs do not cooperate with humans regarding our efforts to substantiate anything about them.

Psychically contributing either possibly real or possibly imaginary data about ETs is one matter, usually only a confusing one. But realizing feedback on even one part of that data is an entirely different matter. And it is a matter in which everyone should take a creative interest. Of what, then, would feedback on UFO-ET matters consist? Here is the principle problem of ufology as a whole – and it is the principle problem also of any attempts to incorporate remote viewing protocols into ufology.

## Summing up

Remote viewing is composed of a five-part protocol, and when any one of the five parts is omitted (such as confirmatory feedback), then what has taken place is something else other than remote viewing. The history of the origin and developments of remote viewing are easily available, and its exact definition is found in several books, documents, and in other sources. Its definition is clearly given in *The Encyclopedia of Parapsychology and Psychical Research* (1991), compiled by Arthur S. Berger and Joyce Berger (although those compilers do not correctly attribute its origin, probably because of the lack of historical data).

To quote that encyclopedia: "Remote viewing: A *protocol* to test for extrasensory perception." (Emphasis added.)

"Testing for" extrasensory perception requires feedback, and as such is the key element regarding remote viewing. Without feedback confirmations only unconfirmed psi perceptions have taken place and should be openly and fairly presented as such. It is not ethical to try to lead others into believing that psi perception has taken place until it can be confirmed by appropriate feedback.

I fully believe that many people have correct psychic intuition, feelings or even hunches concerning UFOs and ETs. I certainly have some of my own, and it is desirable to encourage the wider publication of them – but only as such. If these important definitional boundaries are not understood and maintained, the ultimate result will be an ambiguous definitional quagmire of benefit to no one, and the demolition of what the remote viewing protocol achieved in terms of respect and repute.

I do not excuse myself from this sensible, and ethical, mandate. Since 1971, I've participated in well over a million remote viewing exercises, and rigorously dissected its psi-perceptual processes. But I've never said I was a "remote viewer," or claimed to use "remote viewing" as an ability. Remote viewing is a format, and only the feedback of each separate remote viewing exercise establishes whether or not remote viewing has taken place.

In a very literal sense, then, it is the positive feedback that is remote viewing. Without the former the latter cannot be said to exist, and clearly no utilitarian value of it can be perceived.

## References
Note: Regarding the following references, while remote viewing was originally conceived at the ASPR in 1971, it received international merit after 1974 at Stanford Research Institute (SRI) under the auspices of Dr. H.E. Puthoff and Mr. Russell Targ, along with many other contributors with whom I worked for 18 years, and to whom I'm deeply indebted both in fact and memory.

Additionally, the remote viewing protocol was successfully demonstrated by other research groups. I've listed the following references chronologically, since the chronology takes precedence over the authors in that it shows the increasing involvement of remote viewing with various kinds of wider interests. The full history of the development of remote viewing has yet to be written but is under way by myself.

Swann, Ingo. *To Kiss Earth Good-Bye*. New York: Hawthorn Books, 1975. Republished: New York: Dell Publishing Co., 1977.

Wilhelm, John L. *The Search for Superman*. New York: Pocket Books, 1976. Also, "Psychic Spying?" in *Outlook/Washington Post Sunday Magazine*, August 7, 1977.

Puthoff, Harold E. and Russell Targ. *Mind-Reach: Scientists Look at Psychic Ability*. Delacorte Press/ Eleanor Friede, 1977.

Swann, Ingo. *Natural ESP: The ESP Core and Its Raw Characteristics*. New York: Bantam Books, 1987. Republished: Los Angeles: Jeremy P. Tarcher, Inc., 1991. (Note: This is the only published book discussing and illustrating the most important psychic-mind-dynamic phenomena and problems of the remote viewing process.)

Mitchell, Janet Lee. *Out-of-Body Experiences: A Handbook*. London: McFarland & Company, 1981.

Ebon, Martin. *Psychic Warfare: Threat or Illusion?* New York: McGraw-Hill Book Co., 1983.

Gittelson, Bernard. *Intangible Evidence*. New York: Simon & Schuster, 1987.

Jahn, Robert G. and Brenda J. Dunne. *Margins of Reality*. New York: Harcourt Brace Jovanovich, 1987.

Mitchell, Janet Lee. *Conscious Evolution*. New York: Ballantine, 1989.

Blum, Howard. *Out There: The Government's Secret Quest for Extraterrestrials*. New York: Simon & Schuster, 1990.

Alexander, John B., Richard Grolier, and Janet Morris. *The Warrior's Edge*. New York: William Morrow and Company, 1990.

*Ingo Swann (1933-2013): Psychic, author and visionary artist, especially renowned for his remote viewing experiments.*

FATE September 1993

# Vatican Gives Nod to ETs

## Paola Leopizzi Harris

On May 14, 2008, Father Gabriel Funes, the Jesuit priest who directs the Vatican's observatory at Castel Gandolfo near Rome, declared: "As an astronomer, I continue to believe that God is the creator of the Universe. The search for extraterrestrial life does not contradict belief in God." He added that some aliens might even be innocent of original sin. "How can we rule out that life may have developed elsewhere?" Funes said. "Just as we consider earthly creatures as 'a brother' and 'sister,' why should we not talk about an 'extraterrestrial brother'? It would still be part of creation."

When Funes calls the extraterrestrial "our brother or sister" we are involved in some revolutionary thinking. That statement goes beyond saying that we are not alone in the Universe. To make this statement even more important, the newspaper *Il Osservatore Romano*, the official mouthpiece of the Vatican, released the interview. In the article, Funes stated, "Even if we don't currently have any proof, the hypothesis of extraterrestrial life cannot be ruled out. Just as there is a plethora of creatures on Earth, there could be others, equally intelligent, created by God."

*Monsignor Corrado Balducci, the author, and John Mack at 2003 X-Conference.*

## More than silent approval

With this statement, Funes echoes the words of Monsignor Corrado Balducci, a UFO researcher with many years in the field. Balducci is known to fellow researchers as the "unofficial" voice of the Vatican. At UFO conferences in Italy, Monsignor Balducci, once Vatican Nuncio to Washington, DC, presaged the words of Father Funes when he said: "All is possible. God created us to give praise to Him, as I imagine He created other species to do the same. How can God be glorified without a varied creation?"

For the past 15 years, I lived in Italy very close to the Vatican, and I often dined with Monsignor Balducci at his home. Balducci, who was also an expert demonologist, wanted to open the door to the Catholic study of ufology. Since he was never hindered in this pursuit by Vatican authorities, he felt they had given him their silent approval. With the proclamation of Father Funes, that approval is no longer silent.

I often asked Balducci if he thought that some aliens were demonic. His answer was, "The devil does not need UFOs."

Balducci believes that over the last 150 years, the UFO phenomenon has appeared sequentially and with an increasing and spreading frequency. He made a strong distinction between this phenomenon and manifestations of the paranormal, such as Spiritualism. He believes adamantly there must be creatures between us and the angels on the evolutionary scale. These could be ETs. Humans are at the bottom of the evolutionary ladder because we know the difference between good and evil, and often choose evil.

The Catholic Church will have a difficult time incorporating such beliefs into official dogma. Maintaining official Catholic doctrine may be impossible in the face of an ET disclosure process. This is all unmapped territory.

The Catholic Church has avoided the subject of UFOs for centuries, although UFOs are clearly depicted in Renaissance art, in which the blessed are followed by beams or balls of light.

## Original sin

Unlike Father Funes, who says that humans may be the only creatures with original sin, Monsignor Balducci said in 2004 that Jesus died for the sins of extraterrestrials as well: "Jesus died for all beings in the cosmos. In the sacred Scriptures, He is called King of the Universe at least 66 times. Never underestimate the great mercy or compassion of God, whose grace and compassion surpass all."

Father Funes asserts that original sin refers to the fallen state from which humans can be saved only by God's grace. "If other intelligent beings exist, it's not certain that they need redemption," he said. "[They could] have remained in full friendship with their creator" without committing original sin. If not, extraterrestrials would benefit equally from the Incarnation, in which Jesus Christ, the Son of God, assumed earthly flesh, body and soul in order to redeem humankind. Father Funes called the Incarnation "a unique event that cannot be repeated."

## Church and science

Father José Gabriel Funes has been named by Pope Benedict XVI as the new director of the Vatican Observatory. He will succeed a controversial American, Father George Coyne. Father Funes, an Argentine Jesuit, is already a member of the Vatican Observatory team.

The Vatican Observatory was established by Pope Leo XIII in 1891 to advance astronomical knowledge and to demonstrate the

*Detail of The Annunciation of St Emidus by Carlos Crivelli, 1486.*

Church's support for the physical sciences. Originally it was located at Castel Gandolfo, near the Pope's summer residence. In 1981, because of the smog that obscures viewing of the sky near Rome, the main observatory was moved to Arizona.

The scientific community and the church split more than four centuries ago as a result of the persecution of Galileo, who said that neither the Earth nor the Sun was situated in the center of the universe. In 1633, Galileo was tried for heretical beliefs and forced to deny his theory.

"The church has somehow recognized its mistakes. Maybe it could have done it better, but now it's time to heal those wounds, and this can be done through calm dialogue and collaboration," said Funes.

The reconciliation between science and the church began in 1992 when Pope John Paul declared that Galileo's trial was a "tragic mutual incomprehension."

Is the Vatican looking for ET? With two major observatories and the indication that it's okay to believe in aliens, we can see hints of a revolutionary new policy.

But then Monsignor Balducci has been studying UFOs for years. He has met most of the important American researchers, such as Steven Greer, Dr. John Mack, Whitley Strieber and Dr. Richard Haines. He has had several meetings with Mexico's Jaime Maussan, who saw him in Rome and filmed him in Washington, DC when Balducci gave permission to the Spanish world to embrace the extraterrestrial reality because it does not conflict with the Catholic religion.

In 2003, I accompanied Balducci from Rome to Washington to Steven Bassett's X-Conference, where he received a special award for courage.

## Balducci's views

UFOs fascinate Monsignor Balducci. He gives the benefit of the doubt to those who report unusual phenomena. "We should believe contactees and witnesses who say they see UFOs because it is based on human testimony, as are our Gospels," he says. "Since a great deal of the Catholic faith is based on witness testimony, we must realize how important human testimony is. It would be a tragedy if we began to be suspicious of all people who report that they experienced something unusual, like seeing crafts in the sky."

Balducci recognizes the inevitable theological implications of life on other planets. "Many church fathers addressed the extraterrestrial presence in early philosophical works," he points out. "I think that we need to examine it, then formulate theological and Biblical considerations on the habitability of other planets."

Balducci points out some clear distinctions between UFOs and religious or spiritual phenomena: "We should exclude [ the notion] that angels use spaceships, because they are merely spiritual beings. They are wherever they want to be, and in the rare cases when they show themselves, they have no difficulty in assuming a visible form. We can say the very same thing about dead people."

Marian apparitions are in another category as well: "The Holy Virgin, in the very few cases when she seems to contact humans (very exceptional episodes and to be confirmed in their authenticity), continues to choose other very different ways to transmit to us her maternal affection, her urgencies, her maternal claims, or her sweet reproaches. We need to separate these realities."

## UFOs and the ET Presence

*Flying object in 14th-century tapestry.*

Monsignor Balducci's thinking on UFOs is informed by his work in other fields. "My conclusions come from my research in parapsychology and demonology. There are human testimonies concerning the UFO phenomenon, in particular the abduction phenomenon, which are essential to historical truth and must be considered seriously. These things cannot be attributed to the devil. He does not need UFOs. This has nothing to do with the devil."

Speculation about UFOs and ETs is not spiritually dangerous, says Balducci. "The existence of UFOs is not contrary to one's faith or Catholic Church doctrine. The acronym UFO is used here in a wider sense to include the existence of living beings on other planets. The aim of my intervention and speaking out is to underline that something real must exist in the phenomena, and that this does not conflict at all with Christian religion, and is considered positive, even among theologians."

### All God's creatures

In the May interview done by the Vatican newspaper *Il Osservatore Romano*, Father Funes agrees that the notion of extraterrestrial life "doesn't contradict our faith" because aliens would still be God's creatures. Ruling out the existence of aliens would be like 'putting limits' on God's creative freedom."

Monsignor Balducci and Father Funes are in agreement. They know a phenomenon exists. Although we don't know who the aliens are, it is possible that they are more evolved than man is today. Perhaps we can learn from them.

*Paola Leopizzi Harris: Italo-American photojournalist and investigative reporter in the field of extraterrestrial related phenomena research, and a widely published freelance writer.*

FATE September-October 2008

# The Critters Who Live in Space
## John White

The term "the UFO experience" lumps together a wide variety of dissimilar phenomena but nevertheless ufologists – those scientists who continually study and pursue the UFO enigma – have made enormous strides toward solving the riddle despite public ridicule, insufficient funds, official harassment and even official suppression. They have labored long and hard to crack the riddle, taking even greater "giant steps for mankind" than those of the astronauts.

Now the mountain of evidence offers a number of plausible explanations for UFOs. The UFO experience is complex and no single explanation, even the common notion of interplanetary spacecraft, will cover all of the phenomena. Dr. J. Allen Hynek, perhaps the world's foremost ufologist, noted in his 1972 book *The UFO Experience,* "The solution of the UFO phenomenon ... might not be easy to accept. It might well call for a rearrangement of many of our established concepts of the physical world that will be far greater even than the rearrangements necessary when relativity and quantum mechanics entered our cozy little world."

*Trevor James Constable.*

An important contribution to UFO data comes from Trevor James Constable of San Pedro, California. A merchant marine radio-electronics officer, Constable is a long-time researcher in borderland science, primarily in the traditions of Rudolf Steiner and Wilhelm Reich. Constable claims to have done what thousands of astronomers, biologists and exobiologists may gasp to hear: discovered and photographed extraterrestrial life, right here on earth!

"Not all UFOs are spacecraft from another world," Constable says. "Quite simply, many UFOs are living organisms. They are biological aeroforms living in the sky unknown to official science. I know. I have seen and photographed them."

Astronomer-exobiologist Dr. Carl Sagan of Cornell University, in his testimony before Congress during the 1968 Symposium on Unidentified Flying Objects, said, "A bona fide example of extraterrestrial life, even in a very simple form, would revolutionize biology .... It would be truly immense."

Constable's tacit reply to Sagan is: "The revolution is here."

The full story of this momentous discovery is told in his book *The Cosmic Pulse of Life,* in which Constable claims to "demonstrate conclusively through photographs that they are right down on earth and not out in the farthest reaches of space upon which astronomical telescopes are ranged."

*Constable and his telescope.*

Constable's "they" refers to animals that live in the sky! Pictures of them taken on infrared film show plasma-bodied creatures – organisms, Constable maintains, consisting essentially of heat-substance at the upper border of physical matter. Neither solid, liquid nor gas, these elemental creatures live invisibly like fish in the ocean of atmosphere. They are normally beyond the range of sight for three reasons. First, their native habitat is the stratosphere at distances beyond unaided sight. Second, their native state of existence is in the infrared portion of the spectrum beyond the range of visible light. Last, they propel themselves at extremely fast speeds, sometimes appearing like meteors before disappearing from view. Constable has nicknamed these strange plasma creatures "critters."

Constable claims a series of photographs published in *Pulse* show "a monstrous, diaphanous critter above Mount Wilson Observatory, with the observatory in the picture. But any infrared telescope at work in that building is not going to record such an object because its focus and focal length will 'see' far beyond it."

The critters, consisting of plasma-matter in its most tenuous form – have the capacity to change their density and thereby pass from one level of tangibility to another. Thus, they sometimes do appear in the visible portion of the spectrum where, if seen by humans, they are quickly labeled UFOs – which of course they are. But they are not mechanical spacecraft; they are living creatures.

These amoeba-like aerial fauna will, Constable thinks, someday be categorized as macro-bacteria in the general field of macro-biology. Furthermore, he believes, critters are not the only organisms in the upper atmosphere. It supports a veritable aerial jungle, an idea also suggested by Sir Arthur Conan Doyle in his story, "The Horror of the Heights" and by pioneer investigator Charles Fort.

*A Constable anomaly.*

## The Critters Who Live in Space

Critters range in size from that of a coin to at least a half mile in diameter. As do most plasmas, they give a solid radar return even though fighter pilots don't see them when vectored by ground control to intercept them. They pulsate like all living organisms and when in visible range often emit a reddish-orange glow, thus accounting for the mysterious "foo fighters" of World War II. Although they can change both their form and their density, critters generally are discerned as discs or spheroids. Their diaphanous mica-like structure allows a limited view of their interior. Some have been seen close up on the ground in full physical density.

Since 1957 Constable and his colleague Dr. James O. Woods have taken hundreds of still and motion pictures of critters with the aid of infrared film and filters, a 35mm camera and a Bolex movie camera. Recently they added pictures on both Super-8 color film and videotape to their evidence. When the late Ivan Sanderson, the well-known biologist and Fortean, saw some of these photos, he said, "...they don't look like machines at all. They look to a biologist horribly like unicellular life-forms, complete in some cases with nuclei, nucleoli, vacuoles and all the rest."

Constable, who also is a well-known aviation historian, first wrote about critters in his 1958 book *They Live in the Sky*, under the pseudonym Trevor James. Many ufologists have acknowledged this out-of-print classic as a major contribution, but *The Cosmic Pulse of Life*, based on 17 more years of research, updates the story.

Why hasn't Establishment science followed the lead Constable offered nearly two decades ago? He tried to enlist professional interest but was powerfully rebuffed. Constable looks to Wilhelm Reich's findings on mass neurosis for the major reason. Humanity is pathologically armored, and this armoring includes distorted and repressed perceptions.

Remarks Constable, "The sterile conceptions of mechanistic science are the ultimate expression of this armoring. Organisms in the condition of pure heat – my critters – signal the end of mechanistic cosmology. I attribute to orthodox scientists, no matter what their eminence, a manifest inability to observe accurately. How else can the tiny critters arcing up from the moon's surface, seen on the videotapes made from the orbiting satellite, have been overlooked so long? They are the same things I recorded above the California desert. If I can see these things on my home TV set, while a roomful of normal people similarly see them, what is wrong with the perceptions of NASA people that they cannot see these perfectly objective recordings?"

Constable backs up his own work with scholarly research proving there were many cases of critter sightings by others both here and abroad long before he began photographing them and in some cases before he was born. The most startling record is the ancient cave paintings at Lascaux, dating from 30,000 to 10,000 BCE. These show, Constable argues, "discs, doughnuts, large fusiform shapes accompanied by lines of small discs ... a collection of shapes indistinguishable from many UFOs reported and photographed in the 20th century."

If Constable is right, his book and his work will be epochal. I am tempted to compare *The Cosmic Pulse of Life* with the works of Einstein and Velikovsky, so revolutionary does it seem to me. One man, working without official sanction and funding, may have done what thousands of scientists backed by billions of dollars haven't been able to do. Apparently, he has made a fundamental breakthrough in ufology and discovered and photographed organisms living in our atmosphere and on the moon. Is it unreasonable to ask science to examine this claim?

## Excerpt from "The Horror of the Heights" by Sir Arthur Conan Doyle (1913)

"Suddenly I was aware of something new. The air in front of me had lost its crystal clearness. It was full of long, ragged wisps of something which I can only compare to very fine cigarette smoke. It hung about in wreaths and coils, turning and twisting slowly in the sunlight. As the monoplane shot through it, I was aware of a faint taste of oil upon my lips, and there was a greasy scum upon the woodwork of the machine. Some infinitely fine organic matter appeared to be suspended in the atmosphere. There was no life there. It was inchoate and diffuse, extending for many square acres and then fringing off into the void. No, it was not life. But might it not be the remains of life? Above all, might it not be the food of life, of monstrous life, even as the humble grease of the ocean is the food of the mighty whale? The thought was in my mind when my eyes looked upward, and I saw the most wonderful vision that ever man has seen. Can I hope to convey it to you even as I saw it myself last Thursday?

"Conceive a jellyfish such as sails in our summer seas, bell-shaped and of enormous size-far larger, I should judge, than the dome of St. Paul's. It was of a light pink color veined with a delicate green, but the whole huge fabric so tenuous that it was but a fairy outline against the dark blue sky. It pulsated with a delicate and regular rhythm. From it there depended two long drooping, green tentacles, which swayed slowly backwards and forwards. This gorgeous vision passed gently with noiseless dignity over my head, as light and fragile as a soap-bubble, and drifted upon its stately way.

"I had half-turned my monoplane, that I might look after this beautiful creature, when, in a moment, I found myself amidst a perfect fleet of them, of all sizes, but none so large as the first. Some were quite small, but the majority about as big as an average balloon, and with much the same curvature at the top. There was in them a delicacy of texture and coloring which reminded me of the finest Venetian glass. Pale shades of pink and green were the prevailing tints, but all had a lovely iridescence where the sun shimmered through their dainty forms. Some hundreds of them drifted past me, a wonderful fairy squadron of strange unknown argosies of the sky – creatures whose forms and substance were so attuned to these pure heights that one could not conceive anything so delicate within actual sight or sound of earth.

"But soon my attention was drawn to a new phenomenon – the serpents of the outer air. These were long, thin, fantastic coils of vapor-like material, which turned and twisted with great speed, flying round and round at such a pace that the eyes could hardly follow them. Some of these ghost-like creatures were twenty or thirty feet long, but it was difficult to tell their girth, for their outline was so hazy that it seemed to fade away into the air around them. These air-snakes were of a very light grey or smoke color, with some darker lines within, which gave the impression of a definite organism. One of them whisked past my very face, and I was conscious of a cold, clammy contact, but their composition was so unsubstantial that I could not connect them with any thought of physical danger, any more than the beautiful bell-like creatures which had preceded them. There was no more solidity in their frames than in the floating spume from a broken wave.

"But a more terrible experience was in store for me. Floating downwards from a great height there came a purplish patch of vapor, small as I saw it first, but rapidly enlarging as it approached me, until it appeared to be hundreds of square feet in size. Though fashioned of some transparent, jelly-like substance, it was none the less of much more definite outline and solid consistence than anything which I had seen before. There were more traces, too, of a physical organization, especially two vast, shadowy, circular plates upon either side, which may have been eyes, and a perfectly solid white projection between them which was as curved and cruel as the beak of a vulture.

"The whole aspect of this monster was formidable and threatening, and it kept changing its color from a very light mauve to a dark, angry purple so thick that it cast a shadow as it drifted between my monoplane and the sun. On the upper curve of its huge body there were three great projections which I can only describe as enormous bubbles, and I was convinced as I looked at them that they were charged with some extremely light gas which served to buoy up the misshapen and semi-solid mass in the rarefied air. The creature moved swiftly along, keeping pace easily with the monoplane, and for twenty miles or more it formed my horrible escort, hovering over me like a bird of prey which is waiting to pounce. Its method of progression – done so swiftly that it was not easy to follow – was to throw out a long, glutinous streamer in front of it, which in turn seemed to draw forward the rest of the writhing body. So elastic and gelatinous was it that never for two successive minutes was it the same shape, and yet each change made it more threatening and loathsome than the last.

"I knew that it meant mischief. Every purple flush of its hideous body told me so. The vague, goggling eyes which were turned always upon me were cold and merciless in their viscid hatred. I dipped the nose of my monoplane downwards to escape it. As I did so, as quick as a flash there shot out a long tentacle from this mass of floating blubber, and it fell as light and sinuous as a whiplash across the front of my machine. There was a loud hiss as it lay for a moment across the hot engine, and it whisked itself into the air again, while the huge, flat body drew itself together as if in sudden pain. I dipped to a *vol-piqué*, but again a tentacle fell over the monoplane and was shorn off by the propeller as easily as it might have cut through a smoke wreath. A long, gliding, sticky, serpent-like coil came from behind and caught me around the waist, dragging me out of the fuselage. I tore at it, my fingers sinking into the smooth, glue-like surface, and for an instant I disengaged myself, but only to be caught around the boot by another coil, which gave me a jerk that tilted me almost on to my back.

"As I fell over I blazed off both barrels of my gun, though, indeed, it was like attacking an elephant with a pea-shooter to imagine that any human weapon could cripple that mighty bulk. And yet I aimed better than I knew, for, with a loud report, one of the great blisters upon the creature's back exploded with the puncture of the buckshot. It was very clear that my conjecture was right, and that these vast, clear bladders were distended with some lifting gas, for in an instant the huge, cloud-like body turned sideways, writhing desperately to find its balance, while the white beak snapped and gaped in horrible fury. But already I had shot away on the steepest glide that I dared to attempt, my engine still full on, the flying propeller and the force of gravity shooting me downwards like an aerolite. Far behind me I saw a dull, purplish smudge growing swiftly smaller and merging into the blue sky behind it. I was safe out of the deadly jungle of the outer air.

"Once out of danger I throttled my engine, for nothing tears a machine to pieces quicker than running on full power from a height. It was a glorious, spiral vol-plane from nearly eight miles of altitude – first, to the level of the silver cloud bank, then to that of the storm cloud beneath it, and finally, in beating rain, to the surface of the earth. I saw the Bristol Channel beneath me as I broke from the clouds, but, having still some petrol in my tank, I got twenty miles inland before I found myself stranded in a field half a mile from the village of Ashcombe. There I got three tins of petrol from a passing motor car, and at ten minutes past six that evening I alighted gently in my own home meadow at Devizes, after such a journey as no mortal upon earth has ever yet taken and lived to tell the tale. I have seen the beauty and I have seen the horror of the heights and greater beauty or greater horror than that is not within the ken of man."

*John White: Author, educator and lecturer in the fields of consciousness research and higher human development; former director of education for The Institute of Noetic Sciences, founded by Apollo 14 astronaut Edgar Mitchell to study human potential for personal and planetary transformation.*

FATE August 1976

# UFOs, The Universe and Mr. John M. Cage
## James W. Moseley

Some years ago, Lincoln Barnett wrote a book called *The Universe and Dr. Einstein*. John M. Cage, an alert 75-year-old scientist and inventor from Montclair, New Jersey, doesn't claim to be the theoretical mathematician that Einstein was but his thoughts about the simple arithmetic of the General Field Theory raise some interesting questions indeed.

Mr. Cage offers a revolutionary new theory of what makes the Universe go around for one thing. And equally significant, this theory, if it turns out to be valid, could explain the mysteries of UFOs – the flying objects that have been reported from all over the world for centuries.

Since anyone who challenges Einstein is a brave man indeed, the first question we ought to ask is: "Who is John M. Cage?"

He's about as far from a backyard mechanic as one can get. Even though he's not a college-trained engineer, John M. Cage is an original thinker, with many patents to his credit and a long life of accomplishment.

He was loaned to the British Admiralty during World War I to help solve the submarine problem. He invented the hydrophone to detect submarines and designed the type of hydrophone used in the English Channel. He was honored by the British Government for this work.

With Col. E. E. Wilcox, he developed a lightning prevention system adopted by Pan American Oil Company at its enormous tank farm outside Los Angeles. Though considered radical at the time, this system is now thoroughly accepted.

Cage also designed and supervised the building of electronic dehydrators for the Pan American refineries in Southern California that were new and unorthodox at the time but are today recognized as among the most efficient in the industry.

He also designed and built the first radio sets able to plug directly into alternating house current.

Cage has fully allowed patents for devices held secret by the War Division of the US Patent Office. Recently he has been working on devices which will "see through" fog.

This is the man who is challenging some of Dr. Einstein's theories.

Philosophically, Einstein chose to base his beliefs about the universe primarily on the behavior of light rays. When he found that light rays did not appear to travel through space in a straight line, he concluded that the universe itself was round. And when he saw that light disappears if it exceeds a "maximum speed" of 186,000 miles per second, he concluded that matter and energy would disappear, too, if they exceeded that speed.

Recent work on the physics of light rays indicates, however, that Einstein may have been mistaken. In the first place, the experiments that "proved" light rays are curved are unsatisfactory from many points of view. The "proof" was that certain stars could be seen from the Earth even though they were hidden by an eclipse of the sun. Einstein said this meant that the light rays travelled in an arc wide enough to take them around the sun on their way to Earth.

There are several perfectly reasonable alternatives to this assumption. Mr. Cage believes the most logical explanation of the phenomenon is that light rays behave differently in the immediate vicinity of the sun than they do in outer space, because the heavily charged electrostatic field of the sun actually bends them en route, thus enabling us to see the light of stars "hidden" behind the sun.

In the second place, it now is known that light rays can travel faster than Einstein's maximum under certain conditions and that the energy produced by the passage of light through space in excess of 186,000 miles per second may very will furnish the "fuel" for some spaceships of the future. This fact alone proves that the universe cannot be explained by a theory based solely by the behavior of light rays.

For John Cage, the entire universe is underlain with an inherent energy now called "negative" electricity and is the only one that really exists; what we call the "positive" charge is only the absence of the "negative" charge, something like a vacuum or temporarily unfilled space within the fabric of the universe. The power created by the movement of "negative" electricity into these "positive" areas creates what Mr. Cage calls an electrostatic field. This field is permanent and constant; its strength is determined by the amount of "negative" electricity available for transfer to the "positive" areas, and the relative position of matter within the universe is determined by the charge of "negative" electricity it contains.

Within our solar system, for example, the further a planet is from the sun the more its "negative" charge must be. If you could change the negative charge, you automatically would force the planet to move anywhere you might want to put it in relation to the other planets and to the sun.

Another good illustration of the workings of the electrostatic theory is the relationship of the moon and the tides. It is generally thought that tides are caused by the attraction of the moon as it passes over the surface of the ocean. This theory is belied by the fact that the tidal swells do not occur directly beneath the moon. Instead, there is a large swell under the outer edge of the moon in the direction in which it is travelling; and a smaller one that follows beneath the path of the moon and a little to the rear.

John Cage's explanation of these phenomena is that the moon, instead of attracting the ocean waters, pushes them away. This is entirely in accord with the electrostatic theory, which teaches that the moon is where it is because its charge of negative electricity repels it from the Earth. The people who believe that the moon causes tides through attraction cannot explain why the tides are not directly beneath the moon; John Cage's theory can.

It may be that this discussion of scientific theory will seem a trifle academic, but it is only through the electrostatic concept that we can understand Cage's ideas about Unidentified Flying Objects.

John Cage suggests the enigmatic "UFOs" are not machines, as most people seem to believe, but are "sentient life forms of a highly tenuous composition, charged with and feeding upon energy in the form of negative electricity." As such the saucers might best be described as life fields, not as objects at all.

These life fields, it is theorized, came into being the same way as all other living things, but their environment forced them to modify their evolutionary development so as to make them incapable of wandering into areas of high gravity for long periods. The UFOs are not, however, space animals in the usual sense of the word. They represent a life form that diverged from the evolutionary process of this planet at such an early age that they do not fall into any predetermined category established for the classification of ordinary terrestrial life forms.

The characteristic behavior of the UFOs in relation to aircraft was noted from the earliest days of aviation. They would frequently swoop down from the heavens and trail along after the aircraft, much as a dolphin follows a ship.

They may be displaying conscious intelligence in engaging in aerial circus tactics. In one of their favorite maneuvers, one opponent races headlong toward the other, only to turn away at the last possible moment. The "saucer beings" frequently have been observed at this and other sports; perhaps when they see an airplane they believe it to be another species of upper atmosphere creature and hence seek to engage it in the contest – sometimes with tragic results for both.

Of course, Mr. Cage is by no means the originator of the "life field" theory. His contribution to the solution of the UFO mystery lies in his suggestion that the saucers "feed" on negative electricity. This theory explains such difficult questions as motive power, procreation and the fact that UFOs apparently are able to appear and disappear at will and to assume an infinite number of shapes, sizes and color schemes. The saucers, according to Cage's point of view, contain a natural mechanism for the absorption and discharge of negative charges until they have reached their capacity. Then, in the attempt to discharge their overloaded systems, they go through the fantastic gyrations and aeronautic peregrinations that have been a familiar feature of many UFO "sightings."

This would clarify also the "mother ship" phenomenon, where smaller UFOs (the young of the species?) are seen retreating to their mother's side, much like the marsupials of Earth. The more we think of the UFOs as intelligent living beings whose lives are governed by many of the factors that govern our own lives, the more the missing parts of the puzzle fall into place.

If the UFOs really are living creatures, how will their lives be affected by the age of space? The repeated malfunction and even disappearance of many relatively simple mechanical satellites may be closely related to the answer. The ability to draw out the negative ions of the satellite structure would give them the power literally to disintegrate the materials used in our vehicles. It would be unfortunate if they should decide they don't like us. We haven't really taken up much of their *lebensraum* yet, but the future may be different.

The earliest modern suggestion that UFOs were living things came from the Father of Ufology, Charles Fort. His disciples were quick to elaborate on these theories and one of the most distinguished of them, the Countess Zoe Wassilko Serecki, did so in an article published in the important European occult journal *Incomnue* in 1955.

This article, in turn, came to the attention of a prominent American Fortean scholar, Ivan T. Sanderson, a zoologist and author who makes his home in New York City. Writing in 1957, Mr. Sanderson summarized the Austrian countess' theory as meaning that "life forms fed on pure energy, dwelt in space, and constructed bodies for themselves out of tenuous bladders of colloidal silicones. Colloids exist between the solid and the liquid states, and sooner or later, among these colloids certain combinations of elements in certain mixtures must come together. These are of a nature that automatically combine to produce ever more complex substances ending in what chemists call proteins."

Collateral and complementary to Cage's electrostatic theory is his advocacy of etherian physics. In his system, the sum total of the negative electricity present within the universe is united in a common bond, called the "ether."

The ether is broken only by electrostatic fields which have achieved a sufficiently powerful charge of negative electricity to prevent the dispersion of their energies into the general area of space. This means, of course, that space is not empty although the electrostatic fields within it are many times denser than space itself. Matter and energy behave differently in an electrostatic field than they do in space, with the result that something that is true on Earth might not hold true for outer space.

For example, Mr. Cage teaches that the rays of the sun have no inherent properties of their own and that the sensation of heat which we derive from them is the result of an interaction between certain rays emitted by the sun and the electrostatic field surrounding the Earth. Space is not the cold, dark hole it is often thought to be. The ether of space, having at least a mild negative charge, must interact with the rays of the sun to produce at least a modicum of warmth.

The same can be said about some regions in our own upper atmosphere. More is being learned on this score with every passing day, and it already is evident that certain "belts" of the upper regions may provide their inhabitants with an environment far different from that imagined by many. It is not unlikely that there are places in the high altitude range that enjoy a climate much like Florida's.

The conclusion that the "saucer beings" travel by means of negative electricity inevitably suggests that those of us who are not blessed with the natural equipment to survive life in the upper atmosphere might, nevertheless, be able to construct a spacecraft that would operate on similar principles. John Cage's efforts to minimize the effects of gravity through the creation of an electrostatic field have met with some success in the laboratory.

A Cage saucercraft could be airborne within a very few years. Presumably it would be constructed of a light plastic material with a metallic base and would contain no moving parts in its mechanism other than those required to steer the machine and to regulate the flow of negative particles to and from the electrostatic field.

It should be emphasized that this proposal has nothing in common with "free energy" schemes but is based on well-established principles of physical science which have been ignored of late because they lack the glamour of their more spectacular competitors in the field of space propulsion systems.

Although the Cage saucercraft would not feature free energy it would be powered by a fuel available throughout the known universe, as opposed to an alternative system based on light propulsion and electromagnetic oscillation devices.

Instead of trying to break the space barrier, we should devote some attention to the possibility of reaching the stars simply by riding the crests of the electrostatic waves traversing the entirety of the cosmos.

This is the real New Frontier of our Age, and John Cage may be among its foremost pioneers.

*James W. Moseley (1931-2012): Author and commentator on UFOs, publisher of* Saucer News *and* Saucer Smear. *Moseley both exposed UFO hoaxes and created some of his own.*

FATE September 1962

# Are UFOs Alive?

## Brad Steiger

Fay Clark, the publisher of Hiawatha Books, who died on October 23, 1991, was an early mentor of mine. When I was just beginning to seriously explore the strange, the unusual and the unknown, it seemed that Fay knew everyone in the psychic, paranormal and UFO fields from coast to coast. He opened many doors for me – and he opened corners of my mind that might have remained shut far longer if not for his guidance and inspiration.

An extra bonus for me was that Fay was an absolute dead ringer for the great motion picture actor Claude Rains, even to his manner of speaking. Sometimes I truly felt as though I was receiving instruction from the Invisible Man, Sir John Talbot or Mr. Jordan.

I want to share this remarkable account of a UFO sighting, circa 1973, from Fay in his own words:

"I had been investigating UFOs for 22 years, but the sighting that completely changed my view of the phenomenon occurred at Lone Pine, California. My wife and I observed a UFO resting on a small grove of aspen trees. We had been attracted to the area by a terrifically bright light that was so intense we were unable to look directly at it.

"Then the light subsided somewhat and we could see the clear outline of the object. All the way around it were openings in its side. The light began to grow until it covered nearly the entire area of the object. As it grew in size, it lost its brilliance and became a lavender color. When the light reached nearly the entire size of the object, the illumination began to shrink down again until it got to the very brilliant white portion again, which, if my judgment were correct, would probably have been about 20 feet in diameter. Then the light would again increase its size to maybe three-quarters or four-fifths of the size of the entire object, and it would be that lavender color.

"This process of expansion and contraction of light continued, and my wife and I realized that it was matching the rhythm of our respiration rate.

"We became aware that the object was increasing its tempo. We saw one edge of the UFO raise so that it was no longer level with the tops of the trees. In the length of time it took me to turn my head, the object had moved 10 miles out over Death Valley. I know it was 10 miles, because we drove out underneath it.

"The thing that really amazed my wife and me was that it took off at that tremendous speed instantly – with no sound, no fire, no smoke. And all the trees leaned with it. They were not blasted backward. We looked the area over carefully and found no more small limbs and leaves on the ground than one would find under any grove of trees.

"The word that kept coming to me was that the object was impelled, rather than propelled. It was drawn, rather than pushed. If there would have been any force pushing it, it certainly would have blasted limbs and leaves off the trees.

"We drove out in the desert and stayed with the object for probably an hour and a half, directly underneath it. When we first stopped the car, some substance that looked like whipped cream or heavy fog rolled out of the openings in its sides. It was probably not over 300 feet above the ground, but it was completely hidden from view after it produced its own "cloud" of this substance.

"We knew it was there, though, so we drove back a distance so that we could clearly see it sitting on top of its artificial cloud.

*Fay Clark.*

## It's Alive!
"What we were observing, I believe, was a phenomenon going on inside the object. I believe that the thing was breathing, and I see no reason to change my thought on that matter.

"My wife and I both had the feeling that we were witnessing the ultimate in creation. The closer we came to the object, the more we were suffused with a feeling of reverence and beauty and humbleness.

"I'll tell about another object we witnessed, and I will illustrate why I know there were no occupants inside it. This sighting occurred outside of Seligman, Arizona. We watched the object coming, then observed it change its course to come to hover not more than 15 feet above our Volkswagen. It seemed to me that it was just looking at us, as if it were studying our little car.

"I jumped out with my Hasselblad camera and swung it up to take a picture. But before I could even touch the shutter, the UFO zipped right toward a little butte.

"I had a terrible, sick feeling that anything so beautiful was going to crash and be destroyed. Instead of crashing, though, just before it touched the butte it shot straight up. It didn't stop; it just changed direction – a right angle, straight up – and disappeared.

"No crew could have been in any craft and survived such a maneuver. They would have been mashed against the sides of the vehicle, then pulled apart by the acceleration straight up.

"I do not believe that we observed a craft made by beings from some other planet. I believe that we were watching a living creature, a form of life that moves into our dimension.

"Different people throughout the years have said to me, 'Fay, you know a lot more than you are telling. Come on now, tell us the truth. Admit that you made contact with the aliens inside the object. At least tell us they contacted you.'

"But, Brad, we were not contacted; and there were no occupants inside the object. We only had the most wonderful feeling of peace and harmony, and the knowledge that we were witnessing the beauty of the ultimate of creation.

"I firmly believe that UFOs are a form of life that come not from another planet but from another dimension. I believe that they are probably all around us all the time – just outside of our own dimension.

## Extradimensional forms

"When I discussed the matter of living UFOs with another old friend, Trevor James Constable, he said that biological life in the upper octave of terrestrial existence has been overlooked by too many UFO investigators who early on were in favor of the foregone conclusion that UFOs were vehicles from outer space.

"T.J. handed me a stack of photos of UFOs that he had taken with a Leica G IR 135 infrared film at f3.5, 1/30.

"'These are plainly biological forms,' he said. 'These are plasmic living organisms native to our atmosphere. As they appear in these photographs, they give one the impression of looking through the side of an aquarium.'

## Barometric pressure wave

"Constable continued: 'The daily etheric breathings of the Earth produce a barometric pressure wave twice daily, which formal science has never been able to explain. There is enough energy in these barometric waves to run the world's machines – if we can but find the transducer. The torque drive of the Earth itself is an inexhaustible, life-positive energy source of staggering magnitude. That's what civilization depends on – making material substance spin. We see the discs in our skies manifesting these spinning motions over and over again, pressed down upon us in such profusion that one wonders how there can be any vestige of skepticism remaining. Wilhelm Reich has already shown that motors can be run directly from the cosmic life energy, or orgone, as he discovered and refined that energy.

"'The characteristic of this coming epoch – heralded by UFOs – is that free primary energy will run the world. No one can put etheric force into a wire and sell it. No sheik can say that tomorrow etheric force is going to cost four times what it does today. No one can confine it within storage tanks and demand money for it. Everyone is going to have energy to do the world's work without pollution and without financial price.

"'Before long, someone will uncover that all-important step (discovered by Wilhelm Reich but not disclosed by him) by which etheric force can be transduced into existing electric motors or simple adaptations of them. Orgone and magnetism are cheek by jowl. The UFO evidence screams this at the world. The era of free primary energy is imminent, and its imminence is reinforced by the absolute necessity for its appearance. The UFO shows the feasibility and potential of etheric force in technological use. With etheric force comes not just a new technical epoch, but a cultural and educational change forced by the need to understand etheric energies as we now understand other energy forms.

"'The price for this new technical epoch is a forced overhaul of our whole mode of existence. We will see the beginning of a reunion between science and religion as the cosmic energies – pervaded with life and themselves the milieu of living beings – come into technical utility. Man will find the central parts of his own physical existence inseparably bound up with etheric energies, and he will be opened to a widened understanding of himself and the cosmos that produced him. The ultimate consequence will be a new humanity.'"

*Brad Steiger: Writer, author and frequent contributor to* FATE.

FATE September-October 2010

# Personalities

# The Men Who Ride in Saucers

## Max B. Miller

"I am Mon-Ka. I am speaking to you from the Planet Mars."

These words did not sound incredible to the 2000 delegates who attended the first national convention of the Amalgamated Flying Saucer Clubs of America at the Los Angeles Statler Hilton last July 11-12 [1959]. These words were no stranger than any of the others uttered by approximately 45 speakers who all claimed to be in contact with the space people who operate flying saucers.

"Mon-Ka" is actually a voice – one of many, in fact – on tape recordings. Richard T. Miller (no relation to the writer), an unemployed electronics technician, says he has been in contact with the space people since 1954.

At first, Miller related, Mon-Ka and other "space beings" projected their messages directly onto sealed reels of tape via a "tensor beam." Later, however, they decided to use Miller as a "medium," and they are still utilizing his vocal chords while he supposedly is in a trance. The Mon-Ka voice sounds much as if Miller were making his own voice sound a few years older.

*Richard T. Miller, another principal speaker at the convention, displays model of saucer. He has formed the Solar Cross Foundation to distribute tapes claimed to contain messages from space people, such as "Mon-Ka" of the planet Mors.*

The Dick Miller tapes, as they are called, have gained such popularity that Miller has founded the Solar Cross Foundation in association with Harry "Gayne" Myers, a Hollywood high school teacher. Their claimed objective is to distribute these taped "messages" (at $4.50 per copy) to spread the word of the space people. The space men on tapes, however, never have anything very specific to discuss. Primarily they warn that world conditions are becoming strained and that nuclear bomb tests should be terminated, lest worse come to worst.

But Miller's messages are no more no less credible than those from George King, who came from London to speak at the historic convention. Promptly at 10 AM on July 12, King stood up before a large audience in one of the six auditoriums provided for the convention speakers and donned a pair of dark goggles.

King's young and uniformed assistant rose to quiet the excited throng. "No one may enter or leave or move about during the experiment." His deep British accent echoed slightly to the vast auditorium. "And no flash pictures, please."

George King bowed his head as a hush fell over the audience. After several moments his head jerked up. "This is the 20th sector of the Planet Mars speaking." The voice was strong and commanding and, like Mon-Ka, warned against continued A-bomb detonations by the nations of earth.

George King is a thin, balding middle-aged gentleman who seldom smiles. He has founded the Aetherius Society in London to promulgate his messages from the space visitors.

"I knew some years ago that I had come to earth with a special mission to perform – had been specially chosen for some great spiritual task," King writes in *Cosmic Voice*, a small periodical he has no difficulty in selling for 50 cents a copy. "The words of Jesus still burn through my brain like the flames of some Sacred Fire, to urge me ever onwards."

The Aetherius Society is currently sponsoring an unusual project they call "Operation Starlight." Members of the Society go on regular junkets to certain mountains around the world to "charge" them. As only members of the sect will be told when the end of civilization approaches, they can go to the "charged" mountains where they will be "saved." The Aetherius Society claims that Mr. King "quite definitely... is the only individual on earth who is able to perform this mighty and unprecedented feat" of charging mountains with spiritual energy.

Convention Chairman Gabriel Green, who quit his job with the Los Angeles Board of Education to devote full time to this "movement," must take credit for an orderly if not exceptionally well-organized gathering – one that most delegates believed to be eminently successful. But while the surface was smooth, the undercurrents were troubled.

Kevin Rowe, a bulldozer operator who claims to have been to outer space more than 350 times, told conventioneers that "there are more liars in the flying saucer field than anywhere else." (Rowe, incidentally, maintains that an "eighth-dimensional force field" surrounding the earth will prevent any terrestrial rockets from hitting or going beyond the moon.)

Dan Martin of Detroit claimed that 99 percent of the other convention speakers were frauds. "The public is tired of all these fantastic stories," he declared and then went on to say that he was lifted into a Venusian space ship with a crew of Mercurians "on a ray that neutralizes gravity." He was given a lunch of fruit salad and wine.

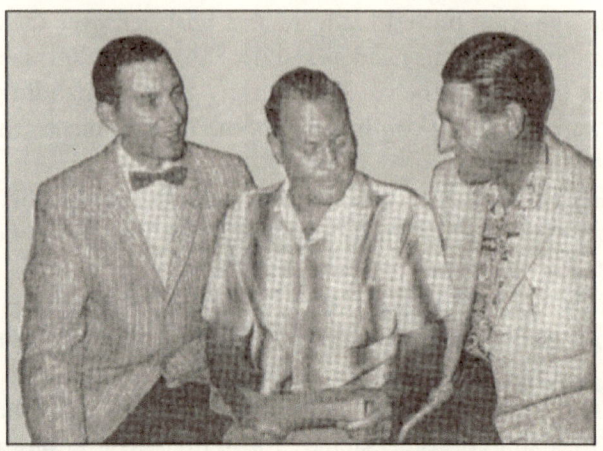

*Among principal speakers at the convention in Los Angeles were (left to right) Gabriel Green, Director of Amalgamated Flying Saucer Clubs of America; Daniel W. Fry, author; and Kelvin Rowe, saucer "contactee." All photos by Max B. Miller.*

Dan Martin also alleges that the earth will turn on its axis in 1964 when a nuclear explosion breaks up the arctic ice cap. He says the space people then will land and – in Red Cross fashion – then help devastated earthlings.

A highlight of the ASFCA convention was the appearance of the self-styled "Dr. Rev." William Suther. Suther is a dynamic and surprisingly confident 16-year-old boy from Chicago who claimed that the space people from another universe – the "ultra-violet universe" – have designated him to unite the children of the world to save humanity.

William Suther (he refuses to be called "Bill") has only contempt for adults, claiming that they have caused all the world's problems. His undisputed popularity at the weekend gathering would indicate that he was superior to the other speakers, and for that matter, to his audience as well.

But Rowe, Martin, King, Suther and Company were still outranked by Prince Neosam, a self-styled visitor from the Planet Tythan, eight-and-one-half light years distant. Prince Neosam, who says his "earth name" is Lee Childers, claims to be 251 years old. He says his body was turned into that of a baby and deposited on a doorstep 31 years ago.

*Orfeo Angelucci, convention speaker and author, displays newspaper headline. He said he was contacted by the flying saucer people in 1953.*

Princess Neosam, or Mrs. Lee Childers, is an attractive woman with an engaging personality. But she doesn't look quite 241 years of age. (Come to think of it, why would any woman claim to be 241 years old?)

Lee Childers predicted that a shift of the earth's axis should destroy our civilization within a year. (Now is the time for all red-blooded young men to take out life insurance.) And like Dan Martin, Prince Neosam states that the space brothers will help us. Anyone wishing to be saved will be taken aboard space ships, the Prince advises, and you don't have to belong to the Aetherius Society.

The Los Angeles convention was prefaced by some negative publicity directed at the gathering by the National Investigations Committee on Aerial Phenomena (NICAP) in Washington, DC. In a telegraphed statement to Convention Chairman Green, retired Marine Corps Major Donald E. Keyhoe, Director of NICAP, stated:

"NICAP is emphatically opposed to your Los Angeles program, which focuses attention on unproved and often absurd claims of contact with space men. Many of these claims are known to be false. Practically all are regarded with suspicion by the press and general public. Your carnival approach to the subject of unidentified flying objects is sure to cause public ridicule, offsetting serious work by NICAP and their reputable fact-finding organizations."

(NICAP was established in the District of Columbia in 1956 to investigate and evaluate UFO sighting reports. Many of their 5,000 members are airline and military pilots, radar observers, astronomers, physicists and other qualified personnel, although membership is open to anyone. Its Board of Governors includes educators, admirals and generals, including Vice Admiral Roscoe H. Hillenkoetter, a former director of the Central Intelligence Agency. NICAP takes UFO reports seriously but it discounts the "contactees" – those who claim contact with people from other worlds.)

When asked about the NICAP statement at a press conference, Gabriel Green stated that NICAP is doing constructive research and is entitled to its opinion. And NICAP's opinion was decidedly not his opinion. Green hinted that some "sour grapes" may have provoked the condemnation.

Convention speaker Daniel W. Fry was a little more specific. He charged that if Green and his associates were as conservative and narrow-minded as NICAP, flying saucer research would have progressed little in the 12 years since pilot Kenneth Arnold spotted nine shining, saucer-like objects over the Cascade Mountains in Western Washington on June 24, 1947. Fry stated that we have learned all there is to know from UFO sighting reports, and that the next logical step is to evaluate the contact claims. The convention delegates enthusiastically concurred.

Daniel Fry is vice president of the Crescent Engineering Company, in El Monte, California. The company manufactures instrumentation and measuring devices for defense contractors.

Fry claims to have been contacted by a remote-controlled "oblate spheroid" while employed as a blast technician with the Aerojet General Corporation at the White Sands Proving Ground [New Mexico] on July 4, 1950.

The disc purportedly took Fry aboard and whisked its lone occupant to New York and back within 30 minutes – a velocity in excess of 8,000 mph. Unfortunately, Fry had no witnesses.

One perhaps not unexpected "invader" at the convention was "Miss Venus," who occasionally employs the earth name of Angel McCall.

*Exotically garbed Angel McCall was "Miss Venus" at the convention.*

Miss Venus exhibited rhinestone eyebrows, blue face powder, and jewel-tipped eyelashes. She will be featured in the forthcoming musical, *From Venus With Love.*

Gloria Lee Byrd, an attractive young brunette housewife, was not as unorthodox in appearance as Miss Venus, but some of her ideas were certainly unconventional. In a lecture entitled "Saucers, Science and Sex," Mrs. Byrd told her audience that she had been in contact with a Jupiterian named "J.W." since September 1953. They communicate through "automatic writing."

Gloria Lee, a former airline stewardess now married to an aeronautical engineer, claims to have been the instrument by which J.W. wrote *Why We Are Here,* a recently published book offered for sale at the convention. In a chapter on "The Sexual Question," J.W. had some pointed remarks directed to us inhibited earthlings.

"The trouble with the minds of this planet today is you have entirely misconceived your sexual desires," the Jupiterian advises. "Sex is not evil, as so many of you seem to think. This is a necessary vibration in order to sustain the life forces of positive and 'negative' energy that emanate through this planet." But J.W. warns against abortions. "This is really the worst sin there is."

Some of the delegates to this first annual convention of the Amalgamated Flying Saucer Clubs of America were as anomalous as the speakers. This writer was told of ninth-dimensional space ships and of ionized space people out in the California desert. One middle-aged woman related that she received telepathic messages from her "soul mate" each evening as he traveled from planet to planet.

But one lady delegate seemed more conservative than the others, and she engaged me in a discussion on astronomy. I told her of my interest in Mars and its enigmatic canals which astronomers have observed for many decades. The woman seemed objective and intelligent and was quite absorbed in our discussion.

"And how many times," she finally asked, "have you been to Mars?"

FATE February 1960

# George Adamski and the Blustery Day
## Richard W. Heiden

George Adamski was by far the most (in)famous of the flying saucer contactees. Very few of his contact claims included specific details that could be confirmed, or – on the contrary – that could be disproved.

One such claim involved the alleged contact of December 1, 1958. Adamski said that his train from Kansas City to Davenport, Iowa made an unscheduled 10-minute stop just 20 miles outside of Kansas City, and he got out and completed the trip in the waiting flying saucer. Arthur C. Campbell of NICAP [National Investigations Committee On Aerial Phenomena] investigated this. The railroad conductor and two attendants that Campbell obtained statements from said that there was no such stop, nor was the door of the car left open because its design did not allow for closing from the outside. Moreover, the train could not have made up the time. This last point was corroborated by the engineer, fireman and brakeman.

In 1978 I researched another of Adamski's contacts from April 22, 1953. Some information on this was included in a book review I wrote

*George Adamski.*

for the *APRO Bulletin*. The present article includes additional details that have not been published before.

In chapter 7 of *Inside the Spaceships,* Adamski wrote that he had gone to Los Angeles in April 1953. On April 22, he went for another ride in a flying saucer. He first had dinner with Firkon, his Martian friend. Adamski suggested dinner at 7:15 PM and they walked to "a little cafe close by" the hotel. "We had lingered over our meal while Firkon talked," he said. It was probably at least 9 PM when they left the cafe, at which point Adamski noted that "it was a blustery night, but I scarcely noticed the storm."

The records of the US Weather Bureau say otherwise. The fastest wind that evening was only eight miles per hour at 8 PM and even slower as the evening progressed. At 9 PM the wind speed was just four miles per hour; at 10 PM, a mere two miles per hour; at 11PM, three miles per hour; and at midnight, four miles per hour. The Weather Bureau officially designates eight to 12 miles per hour as a "gentle breeze," four to seven miles per hour as a "light breeze," and one to three miles per hour as "light air." So, it was far from blustery.

*Hotel Clark, Los Angeles.*

Adamski wrote that he always stayed at the same hotel whenever he visited Los Angeles but did not name it. However, Laura Mundo, a follower of Adamski who lived in Michigan, wrote that she once met with Adamski at the Hotel Clark.

I stopped by the Hotel Clark later when I was in Los Angeles for a MUFON symposium. The hotel manager informed me that the hotel had been sold in 1961 and again a few months before my visit. He did not know who the previous owners had been, nor where the guest registers from 1953 might be.

However, if George Adamski did not have an actual contact on April 22, 1953, it is entirely consistent with what he himself said five years later, in the spring of 1958. Adamski was speaking to a group that included brothers Ray and Rex Stanford and Bob R. Matthews. Ray Stanford relates the following:

"Adamski actually said, in telling us that he, Lucy McGinnis, Alice Wells and a 'Mr. and Mrs. Black from San Diego' allegedly had experienced a sighting of what was said to have been a huge, long 'mothership.' His comment was, 'Hell! That was the closest I've ever been to one of them things!' Suddenly Adamski's face showed shock at what he realized he had let slip. 'Oh! I mean, of course, excepting when I been inside!'"

No details were given, as to description, but I suspect he, Lucy or Alice would have described such had there been any details worthy of mention, so I wonder if it might have been an oblique view of a lenticular cloud produced by a low-pressure wave over the nearby mountain top.

"I don't recall either Lucy or Alice chiming in to say how amazing the alleged 'mothership' was, but it's possible one of them might have uttered some very brief, assenting remark," Ray said.

In his seminal contact with Orthon in the California desert on November 20, 1952, Adamski claimed to have actually touched the craft – or come within a foot of it before his arm was jerked by the alleged forçefield around it. Yet on that occasion he did not go inside.

Ray Stanford went on to say, "More condemning than that off-the-cuff slipup was the morning when, over his third cup of 'ekknog' (as Adamski pronounced eggnog), he told us he 'never had to have any physical contact with space people' to write what was in the book *Inside the Space-Ships*. Adamski stressed he learned everything by 'a unified state of consciousness' with 'space brothers and their craft.'

"Understandably, people ask me why Adamski confessed those things. Well, I think the answer was that, under the influence of the well-spiked eggnogs, he took compassion on us relative youngsters and was trying to steer us away from his 'saucer crap' into a world of reality. I think maybe he saw us as bright young men (not yet 21) whom he really, deep down in his heart, didn't want to see wasting their lives following his merchandised 'space brother' fantasies."

I am not given to puns, but I cannot help saying that Adamski was "just blowing wind," and not just in regard to the contact of April 22, 1953.

*Richard W. Heiden: Assistant Editor of the* APRO Bulletin *from 1977 until its end in 1988. He started researching George Adamski in 1976.*

FATE September-October 2011

# Long John Nebel: UFO Pitchman

## Timothy Green Beckley

*Long John Nebel paved the way for radio shows such as* Coast to Coast. *He was a pioneer and a giant. When I went to school at the University of Detroit, my professor would comment about Long John. His subject matter was great – his guests superb – and I thank my lucky stars every time I do* Coast to Coast AM *that the world had Long John Nebel.*

George Noory, host, Coast to Coast AM

Step right on up for a taste of what was once the greatest show on earth!

If you think the craze in paranormal broadcasting is something new, guess again. Before *Coast to Coast AM, Ghost Hunters,* and a slew of internet programs devoted to the strange and unknown, there was the Long John Party Line, beamed nightly across 30 states over WOR, a 50,000-watt station whose transmitter stood in the dark along a marshy stretch of the turnpike just outside Carteret, New Jersey.

After all these years, I can no longer hide the truth: pioneer talk show host Long John Nebel was responsible for my low elementary school grades by making me stay up until dawn at least several nights a week.

## King of all pitchmen is born

Born in 1911, the son of a Chicago confectionary salesman, John Zimmerman ran away from home at the tender age of 15, following the divorce of his parents, to join the circus. He had aspirations to don clown makeup but ended up riding a white steed around a single dirt ring in the community of Wisconsin Dells, Wisconsin. While with the "big top," he knocked about the country as a young man honing what was to become his profession, that of the self-ordained king of all pitchmen. While working the midway the lanky Midwesterner, who would come to stand six-foot-seven, adopted his stepmother's maiden name of Nebel (originally spelled Knebel), and encountered his first psychic, a mind reader by the name of Lady Ester.

Decades later, he recalled for his producer Paris Flammonde an approximation of the speller's pitch used to get those circling the ten-in-one shows outside to pass everyone else by and enter their tent:

"Ladies and gentlemen, if you'll just move in a little closer – make way for the lady, sir – I will have the honor of presenting to you the Lamont Brothers' star attraction, the amazing Lady Ester, who will read your mind without the aid of any device electrical or mechanical. Not surprisingly, she is the seventh daughter of a seventh daughter and was born on Halloween, night, etc."

And so John Zimmerman's – now aka Long John Nebel's – tale of the mentalist would, as it turns out, continue to grow with great elaboration, more or less reaffirming itself later in life as he hit the airwaves and long before his successor Art Bell became the "first" paranormal and UFO broadcaster.

Nebel eventually made his way to the East Coast and set up shop as an auctioneer barking out big sales for items that would probably have had permanent residence in a dusty warehouse somewhere. The general manager of WOR Radio attended one of Long John's auctions and was so impressed by Long John's gift of gab that he offered him a slot on the station, which had such a clear signal that it could be heard in some 30 states at night given the right atmospheric conditions. There were even reports of the show having been picked up as far away as Alaska and west of the Rocky Mountains – an unbelievable feat!

Known as The Party Line Show in those early days, Long John hosted some of the most incredible guests the world has ever known. Long John might well have been the first all-night talk show host in America, and certainly he was the first to use the phones to pose questions to his guests in the studio. Initially, it was a one-sided conversation where the caller would ask the guest a question, but only Long John could hear it and then had to repeat it over the air to his guest and his assorted panel of "experts," who all took diverse views on the topic of the evening.

Later on, the beeper system was developed and two-sided conversations went live in all 30 states where John was heard – and we're talking about hundreds of thousands of listeners in a time when everyone normally went to bed long before midnight. Hell, *The Tonight Show* wasn't even on the air yet, and CBS's *Late Show* – which broadcast a full-length movie every night – went off around 1 AM at the latest. It was dead air and dead silence and good night until around 6 AM, when the airwaves started to hum again. And then came Long John and his friends from outer space. America's sleeping patterns would be forever altered – just ask Art Bell and George Noory, whose careers would not have been so easy if it wasn't for Long John.

## Tall tales

And the stories that he aired on a regular basis were as colossal as the man who broadcast them. Perhaps these tales stood even a bit taller, as you will see.

Frankly speaking, Long John never said he believed any of the stories told to him and his audience. "I don't buy that," he relished saying, but he would still use a guest to boost ratings or attract publicity. Long John was the first radio show host to be given a salary of a hundred thousand dollars annually, the equivalent of what Mickey Mantle was making over at Yankee Stadium, just a short subway ride from 1440 Broadway where Long John and crew had moved from their isolated New Jersey dugout. They were now inside the building that housed the WOR transmitter, located two blocks from the then ultra-seedy Times Square. There wasn't anyone he couldn't get to take the elevator up to WOR's sixth floor studio. And his ratings skyrocketed through the roof.

## Famous guests

There was George Adamski, who said he had met Orthon, a long-haired space visitor from Venus, in the desert near Sun City, California. Andy Sinatra (aka the Mystic Barber), who wore an antenna on his head to protect himself, he claimed, from the dreaded vibrations of the negative space people. Nearly everyone agreed that Andy – who maintained he was related to the famous crooner with the same last name – was a complete whack job. And he was, but a nice guy just the same, who also had a reputation for giving the best haircuts in his Brooklyn neighborhood.

Stuart Robb, who was an authority on the prophecies of Nostradamus before anyone else could make such a claim, was also a guest. He was among the first to experiment with the Electronic Voice Phenomenon, picking up the voices of Einstein and Elvis on his reel-to-reel tape recorder. Robb also had plenty of proof that Shakespeare did not write any of the plays credited to him because he couldn't read or write beyond a grade-school level. Stuart said they were penned by none other than Sir Francis Bacon, who needed a "safety net" for his controversial political concepts that would have been frowned upon by

*George Adamski (left) and Long John Nebel.*

Queen Elizabeth. Although such claptrap from Robb was frowned upon by Long John and others, the claims are currently the subject of a big budget motion picture called *Anonymous.*

Then there came Gray Barker, who spoke in hushed tones about Albert K. Bender having been silenced by the Men In Black, and who later published Howard Menger's *From Outer Space to You,* only to have Menger blow off the opportunity to promote the book after deciding to change his story to that of a government conspiracy rather than an outright contact with space beings.

And who could forget The Party Line's regular panelist, a young man by the name of James W. Moseley, publisher of *Saucer News,* who now publishes the satirical *Saucer Smear*? This was in the era prior to his becoming the acknowledged "Court Jester" of ufology.

There were even the mighty visionaries like science fiction's Arthur C. Clarke and the Great One himself, Jackie Gleason, who stopped into the WOR studios to discuss UFOs and voice their skepticism about the long list of contactees Long John often played host to, insisting they were just hoodwinking charlatans and not space travelers of any sort. Gleason, whose collection of paranormal literature is now housed in the University of Miami, once agreed to go for a ride onboard a flying saucer, but I guess the Space Brothers stood him up because he never made it to the far side of the moon, like the man who became Long John Nebel's biggest drawing card claimed he had done.

Howard Menger was for all intents and purposes the East Coast version of George Adamski, except that his accounts seemed a tad more believable. There was at least some scant independent evidence that something unearthly was happening on Menger's property in the Garden State [New Jersey], and his ability to communicate a good story was heads above any of the other contactees, who mostly resided on the West Coast, thus giving Menger an uncluttered field.

The stories being aired nightly became wilder and wilder, having no boundaries. But the listening public ate them up, and Long John became in his own right a shooting star.

## Enter Long John's producer, Paris Flammonde

I first met Paris Flammonde at Jim Moseley's UFO extravaganza held at the Hotel Commodore in Manhattan in June of 1967 to commemorate

*Paris Flammonde (left) and Long Jogn Nebel.*

the 20th anniversary of Kenneth Arnold's "first" UFO sighting near Mt. Rainier, Washington. The affair attracted over 10,000 UFO diehards and was to become the largest gathering of its type in all flying saucer land. The hefty turnout was largely due to Long John's continual hyping of the event and a rare promise to show up in person to say hello to his masses of fans, something he seldom did.

If you lived in the very hip and celebrated Greenwich Village during the 1960s, you might have seen the dashing figure who was Paris Flammonde at some of the popular coffee shops, reading his poetry. "The Minotaur of Washington Square" was a major creative figure in New York's Bohemian district for 25 years. Among the artists and luminaries he rubbed shoulders with were greats like Tennessee Williams, Dylan Thomas, Truman Capote, Pete Hamill, William F. Buckley and *Valley of the Dolls* author Jacqueline Susann.

With his cape, walking stick and confident stride, Paris was a true *artiste* in every sense of the word. When he entered a room, everyone wanted to hear of his latest escapades in the worlds of entertainment and literature. Due to personal circumstances, around 1958 Paris found himself becoming a bit of an ascetic, keeping to himself and spending considerable time writing, reading and listening to the radio in his apartment. Normally, Paris listened to *The Milk Man's Matinee*, a musical interlude show hosted by the eminent Art Ford (Ford later, by "coincidence," became deeply engrossed in the Bermuda Triangle mystery, producing a film on the disappearance of ships and planes there), but this one night twisting the dial Paris happened upon one of Long John's guests totally butchering a poem by John Keats, attributing it to Percy Bysshe Shelley.

"Misquotes irritate me greatly," Paris recounts of the moment that changed his life, "especially when so famous, and particularly when offered with pomposity. Therefore, I scribbled a note to the program voicing my concern and correcting the matter."

Long John was impressed by Paris's communiqué and sent his emissaries to invite him on the program, but Paris refused to accept the offer. Not one to be slighted, Long John attempted to contact the elusive raconteur directly. Says Paris, "One evening I was summoned to the telephone by my landlady sending word that 'Mr. Nebel' was on the telephone, and I went down to pick up the receiver only to hear a familiar radio voice growl, 'Why in the hell don't you want to be on my goddamned show?'"

Thus began a long-term relationship that incorporated many dozens of personal appearances on the program and segued into Paris becoming Long John's producer and even hosting Nebel's now memorable *The Way Out World*.

When *Coast to Coast AM* host George Noory announced that WOR would be picking up the show in the Big Apple, I contacted LJ's "descendant" to remind him that Long John Nebel had been with WOR for years, and suggested he have Paris Flammonde on to pay homage to the broadcast industry's pioneer of the paranormal. George and staff took up the suggestion and immediately arranged an historic on-air meeting of the minds with Nebel's long-time producer. For 10 minutes Noory waxed nostalgic and eloquent in front of over three million listeners on 530 stations about how UFO pitchman Nebel had set the standards long ago for paranormal dissemination. This is what George Noory had to say:

"Now a long time ago, way before there was Larry King, way before there was Art Bell, there was a fellow by the name of John Zimmerman who went by the air name of Long John Nebel. He was a very influential talk show host and he was at our affiliate (WOR). He enticed. He mesmerized. Heard in New York and along the East Coast for years, he was one of the first to deal with anomalous phenomena – UFOs and the strange. He was one of the first to interview George Adamski, who talked about being taken up in a spacecraft. Long John died two months short of his 67th birthday in 1978. When he died, he had huge, massive ratings. It was quite a ride and we are so honored to be on WOR, the station where Long John made his name."

Now of course I knew Long John, but not all that well. I was on his show toward the end of his career, after he had contracted cancer and moved from WOR to NBC and then to WMCA, which later turned out to be a paid religious program. I was on with James Oberg talking about our astronauts and their UFO sightings. Oberg, who at the time worked for NASA, claimed that there were no such sightings, even though I had documented them by going through the thousands of pages of transcripts between the astronauts and Houston ground control.

Another time I stood up for Howard Menger and some of the contactees, and Long John basically said he didn't think much of their stories. They had all been on his show and he thought they probably were all hoaxers. He was not feeling his oats by this time and was getting very cantankerous. He would be in a wheelchair slumped over, but when the mike came alive he perked up and became a lion, even if only for a few hours.

After his passing, his fifth wife and former model Candy Jones (also the subject of a book on how she was a victim of mind control) took over the program and had me on almost every Sunday. As friendly and charming as she was, she was not Long John! The show died out and the listeners went elsewhere – or possibly to sleep early for the first time in several decades.

## A mini-interview with Paris Flammonde

Paris Flammonde and I hadn't stayed in touch since he moved to the countryside of Pennsylvania, though we exchanged emails now and then. Paris had gotten engrossed in the Kennedy assassination and produced a series of books that were hugely respected by those caught up in this conspiracy. But when asked to do an article on Long John Nebel's wacky universe, I felt it impossible not to pump Paris for the inside scoop on the man who made paranormal broadcasting respectable. Here is a bit of our most recent exchange of words:

**Beckley:** Would you say you knew Long John better than anyone else?

**Flammonde:** As you may or may not know, in addition to producing Long John Nebel's Show at WOR for almost five years (over 7,000 hours) and appearing as a regular panelist for over 1,500 hours, I ghostwrote the entire original LJ book, *The Way Out World of LJ*. My signature is coded on the final page. Of course, additionally, I may have been his best friend during those years, knew all his wives and girlfriends, and spent scores of hours off-mike with him. Since those years, I was approached to do his life, by two publishers, but declined.

**Beckley:** Which guests in the realm of UFOs and the paranormal impressed Long John the most? And were there certain aspects of the paranormal he would not discuss?

**Flammonde:** First, neither of us ever regarded UFOs and the paranormal in the same, or even allied, categories. Second, John was the ultimate doubter, and was never impressed; i.e., took in any serious regard, any purported extra-natural phenomena. Keep in mind that he, himself, did a magic act in his earlier days, and, as a longtime pitchman, knew all the switches.

Noting the above, of course, he never regarded any sort of purported ultra-natural exhibition as real, although he admired the expertise of certain people, but they were mostly professional masters of prestidigitation. See chapters 10 and 11 of *The Way Out World*.

There was no aspect of the paranormal John would not discuss. However, there were persons he would not have on the show, but mostly they were persons who had appeared once and either excessively irritated him or were just poor, uninteresting guests. The classic example of this was not in the area of the outré, but was a very fine author of curious novels, James Purdy, who was more monosyllabic than even a fertile imagination could conceive.

Prince Neosam from Tythan was one of the very few others sent packing (although most courteously). George King was half-dismissed and half left in a snit on his final show. And, as I recall, there was another, whose name escapes me, at the moment.

One must understand that after I came with the show as producer, John abandoned selecting guests. I chose them, which he invariably approved on review on the rare occasions he asked who was coming on that night. (I gave him a description note before the show if the person was unknown to him.) The sole exception in all those years was the actor John Gielgud. He said he couldn't interview him, as he didn't know who he was. Long John had many areas of considerable expertise, but neither legitimate theatre nor literature was among them. Of course, he was widely knowledgeable regarding "show business."

**Beckley:** What was your overall impression of Long John?

**Flammonde:** He was unique, outstandingly the best interviewer I ever saw or heard at any time. Perhaps the sole one I ever saw or heard that always was in total control of the exchange; he could not be surprised. Amused, often; amazed, a couple of times; but never caught off-guard.

Long John as a person? I cannot help you there. Not that I don't know enough, but that I know too much. I have many faults; being a gossip doesn't happen to be one of them. I can say this: I saw him in all the earthly moods but can attest that I never heard him lie (of course, tall tales are not included), or be gratuitously unkind. I knew him to be generous and a good friend and very intelligent.

*Timothy Green Beckley: UFO and paranormal pioneer, radio show host, author and publisher of numerous books on everything from rock music to the secret MJ-12 papers.*

FATE September-October 2011

# Perspectives

# Fifty Years of UFOs

## The Editors of FATE

On June 24, 50 years ago, Kenneth Arnold was flying toward Yakima from Chehalis in Washington State. The sky was clear and empty. Suddenly, he saw a bright flash reflected on his plane. Then, to his left, north of Mt. Rainier, he saw "a chain of nine peculiar looking aircraft flying from north to south at approximately 9,500 feet."

Arnold, an experienced pilot familiar with all kinds of flying objects, was puzzled by the unusual-looking craft that apparently had no tails. He observed them for two to three minutes. These craft, soon to be known as flying saucers and later as UFOs, were not the first unidentified flying objects to be seen in this century, but they sparked public interest in a new and lasting way. This was the beginning of the modern UFO era.

To commemorate Arnold's sighting (the subject of the cover story in the very first issue of FATE magazine), we contacted people known for their interest in and dedication to the subject of UFOs. We asked them to tell us what they consider the most important UFO events of the last 50 years. We've printed highlights of their responses here.

## David M. Jacobs

*Associate Professor of History at Temple University, David M. Jacobs is the author of important books on the subject of UFOs and abductions, including* Secret Life *and* The Threat. *His choices:*

- **The establishment of Projects Sign, Grudge, and Blue Book**. The US Air Force's interest in UFOs began soon after the first sightings were reported. After the Air Force set up a series of projects to study the UFO phenomenon, it embarked on a public relations campaign to reassure the public that everything seen in the sky, no matter how unusual, could be identified as a conventional phenomenon. In spite of its efforts, thousands of its sightings remained unidentified. By subsuming research and then not scientifically analyzing the data, it actively prevented the scientific community's engagement with the UFO data for more than 20 years.

- **Rise of the charlatan-contactees**. These highly publicized individuals claimed that they had ongoing familiar contact with benevolent space brothers who were here to help humankind. These people helped perpetuate in the scientific community the idea that UFOs had no legitimacy.

- **Publication of Ed Ruppelt's** Report of Unidentified Flying Objects, *1956*. This was the first book written by a US Air Force insider who detailed the Air Force's efforts to deal with the phenomenon in the early years. It is still used as a valuable resource of primary information.

- **The conversion of J. Allen Hynek**. Starting as a debunker hired by the US Air Force to weed out astronomical sightings, Hynek had access to Air Force data before any other scientists. Although it took him the better part of 15 years, he gradually came to realize that UFOs represented intelligent technology beyond that known on Earth. When he finally "went public" as a

UFO proponent, he quickly established himself as the world's foremost UFO researcher and lent prestige and legitimacy to the subject.

- ***Publication of Budd Hopkins' Intruders: The Incredible Visitations at Copley Woods, 1987.*** Hopkins discovered the reproductive aspect of the abduction phenomenon, the taking of sperm and eggs, and the creation of the hybrids. Therefore, he began the process of unlocking the mysteries of the UFO phenomenon.

- *The MIT Conference, 1992.* This became the largest abduction conference ever held. It brought together more than 80 scientists and academics who presented a myriad of papers on all themes in the abduction field. The conference showed the splits in theory and methodology that have pervaded abduction research and underscored the difficulties in studying the subject. It also demonstrated that a growing body of scientists and academics were willing to study abductions and that a community of abduction scholars was developing, contentious though it may be.

## Budd Hopkins

Budd Hopkins first saw a UFO in 1965. Within a few years he had become actively involved in UFO investigation, and in 1989, he founded the Intruders Foundation, a not-for-profit organization devoted to research and public education concerning the UFO abduction phenomenon. His latest book [as of this writing] is Witnessed! The True Story of the Brooklyn Bridge UFO Abductions.

- *June 1947: The Kenneth Arnold sighting.* Far from being the first UFO sighting, the Arnold case is singled out for several reasons: the credentials of the witness, his ability in clear daylight to make careful calculations of the objects' speed, and most important, the subsequent national publicity and its effect on the press, the public and the Air Force.

- ***July 1952: The Washington, DC radar/visual sightings.*** The worldwide publicity that followed these radar/visual reports of UFOs over the Capitol served to galvanize public interest in the UFO phenomenon and led a nervous US Air Force to redouble its debunking efforts. Unlike the Arnold sighting, hundreds of people witnessed this disturbing display in proscribed air space.

- ***1966: Publication of* The Interrupted Journey *by John G. Fuller, the story of the Betty and Barney Hill UFO abduction.*** Far more important than the abduction itself – we now know that there is a huge number of such accounts that date from before this 1961 incident – is Fuller's publication in sober, factual prose of what we now see as the basic UFO abduction scenario. This extremely well-documented case study includes the idea of missing time, alien reproductive procedures, paralysis, trauma and the efficacy of hypnosis in retrieving the missing time (even though the hypnotist was a skeptic!). Historically, *The Interrupted Journey* is without doubt the most significant book in UFO literature.

- ***November 1989: The "Linda Cortile" abduction case.*** Apparently for the first time, UFO occupants carried out a 3 AM abduction in full view of numerous witnesses. They observed Cortile and three small humanoid figures floating out of a twelfth-story apartment building window and into a hovering UFO. Several political figures of international importance were among the witnesses in a case that approximates the mythical "landing on the White House lawn."

- ***1992: The publication of* Secret Life *by David M. Jacobs.*** In this landmark work of investigation and research, Jacobs was able to describe, virtually moment by moment, the abduction patterns typically followed by UFO occupants, diagramming by frequency and sequence the various physical and psychological procedures they employ.

The net effect of Jacobs's work was to further distance the activities of the UFO abductors from the world of folklore, myth and religion by clearly demonstrating their rational, purposeful nature.

## Bufo Calvin
*Bufo Calvin is a commentator on the paranormal scene, frequently guesting on radio and internet programs. He produces on-line paranormal-related newsletters from his home base in California.*

The most significant events are those that most affect public opinion. For that reason, I'd have to choose the Robertson Panel, which met January 14-17, 1953. This "Scientific Advisory Panel on Unidentified Flying Objects" was convened by the CIA [Central Intelligence Agency], and its report was classified "secret." (It was released to the public in 1966.)

It concluded that UFOs were not "a direct physical threat to national security," but that the belief in them was dangerous! Immediate action was recommended to "strip the Unidentified Flying Objects of the special status they have been given and the aura of mystery they have unfortunately acquired." It proposed a "debunking" program, and suggested, for example, that the Walt Disney Company might be a good partner to produce materials which would reduce the threat of "hysterical behavior and harmful distrust of duly constituted authority."

The Eisenhower administration apparently embraced this plan wholeheartedly. For many years, the government worked to reduce belief in UFOs, and convinced much of the public that there was nothing to them. It is impossible to say how many and what kind of reports were kept private behind the officially-sanctioned "laughter curtain."

## Tim Brigham
*Tim Brigham is the researcher/editor of* The Devil's Advocate, *a newsletter focusing on UFOs and other paranormal phenomena.*

- **Fatima, Portugal, 1917.** This case is perhaps the one that first concretely tied the UFO phenomenon to Marian apparitions and religion. It also demonstrates the absurdity and contradiction we often find upon careful examination of UFO cases. It is a very important case that can tell us a lot.

- **Gulf Breeze, Florida, 1987.** Looking back on this one now, it seems that what really went on in the Gulf Breeze area was likely connected to military activities. This case could be an example of advanced aircraft testing or even psychological warfare experimentation; it doesn't seem explainable as "aliens from space." This case should serve to remind us that there may be a variety of valid explanations for UFOs and that we should be careful that in our search for truth we rely on logic and evidence to sort out the facts and not get caught up in our desire to prove the reality of UFOs when the evidence points in other directions.

## Jerome Clark

*Former FATE editor and columnist Jerome Clark is a ufologist, author of the three-volume* UFO Encyclopedia *and* The UFO Book, *and editor of* International UFO Reporter.

The evidence that UFOs exist as extraordinary phenomena takes many forms, and if sightings by credible witnesses were sufficient to clinch the case, the argument would have ended long ago. It hasn't, of course, and we can expect it to rage into the next century unless, of course, a spacecraft from another world lands on the White House lawn, or someone in a position of authority, such as the President, makes an announcement, or scientists start investigating reports and devoting the proper resources to them.

An example of a rare instance of the latter is the GEPAN investigation of the Trans-en-Provence CE2 (close encounter of the second kind) in France. On January 8, 1981, an old man working in his garden observed the approach of a disc-shaped UFO. When it landed not far from him, he fled up a hill and watched it from that vantage. After a few minutes the object flew off.

At the spot where the UFO came down, investigators from the Gendarmerie reported that they "observed the presence of two concentric circles, one 2.2 meters [seven feet] in diameter and the other 2.4 meters [eight feet] in diameter ... one within the other .... They also show black striations." The officers collected soil samples both from within and without the circles, the latter intended to serve as a control.

GEPAN, then France's official UFO-investigative agency, took over the investigation. Two years later, GEPAN reported on the seemingly inexplicable condition of the leaves: significant weakening of the chlorophyll pigment, nearly instantaneous aging, and other effects. It concluded that there was evidence of the "occurrence of an important event which brought with it deformations of the terrain caused by mass, mechanics, a heating effect and perhaps certain transformations and deposits of trace minerals."

GEPAN head Jean-Jacques Velasco told a reporter that the agency's study of the mechanical forces responsible for such effects led "with relative certainty" to the conclusion that "the object ... could weigh between four and five tons." Studies continued for years afterward could find no alternative to the conclusion that a machine of unknown origin had come down in a field in the south of France and left puzzling evidence of its presence.

## Scott Corrales

*Scott Corrales's articles about UFOs in Latin America appear frequently in FATE. Here, he discusses four of the most important UFO events outside the United States.*

- *The Antonio Villas-Boas Abduction (Brazil, October 5, 1957)*. The earliest abduction report to be acknowledged by UFO investigators at the time, and one of the first instances of cooperation between US and Latin American experts on the abduction question.
- *The UMMO Hoax (Spain and France, 1965-1994)*. For almost 20 years, Spanish and French researchers received correspondence from the terrestrial agents of an extraterrestrial society known as UMMO, becoming the longest running hoax in ufology. The UMMO hoax shows that it is possible to defraud serious researchers over a prolonged period of time.

- *Valentich Disappearance (Tasmania, October 21, 1978).* Frederick Valentich vanished in mid-flight over the Tasman Sea while being pursued by a UFO. This incident furnished a complete transcript of pilot-to-ground communications up to the moment the unfortunate pilot disappeared.

- *The Black Triangles Appearances (Belgium, 1991-1992).* This latest UFO "configuration" manifested itself repeatedly over Belgian skies, causing the government to make overtures toward civilian ufologists in hopes of enlisting their aid.

## Ann Druffel
*Ann Druffel has been involved in UFO research and writing since the 1950s. Her many publications include* The Tujunga Canyon Contacts *(1980), cowritten with* FATE's *late columnist D. Scott Rago.*

The most important event in the past 50 years of UFO research was the emergence of skilled, motivated individuals and groups of individuals who, collectively or singly, sought to unravel this serious scientific problem. These efforts began with Donald E. Keyhoe (USMC, Ret.), the original "Dean of Ufology," who wrestled privately with the problem at first. Then, from 1957-1970 he directed the National Investigations Committee on Aerial Phenomena (NICAP), a large, influential group of investigators and researchers who combined their efforts to study UFOs. At its peak, NICAP was 15,000 strong and produced several invaluable books on the subject, in addition to Keyhoe's own five books.

NICAP was destroyed in 1970. The UFO field was left in chaos, but new civilian research groups such as the Mutual UFO Network (MUFON) and Center for UFO Studies (CUFOS) filled the void.

## John A. Keel
FATE *columnist John Keel has written about unusual phenomena for more than five decades.*

Peacetime military officers are not particularly distinguished for their executive ability, but the sorry bunch who mishandled the UFO "problem" from the 1940s onward should get a major booby prize. Somehow, they always managed to say or do the wrong thing at the wrong time, and kept the controversy churning by enraging the general public and driving the small coterie of UFO advocates into paranoid fits.

For example, in 1949 they chose to release the totally absurd (and very expensive) Project Grudge report. A few months earlier, a major weekly magazine with a circulation in the millions, the *Saturday Evening Post*, had published a lengthy, two-part article by a top journalist named Sidney Shalett. He had carefully investigated the existing "flying saucer" evidence and interviewed the major participants, including Ray Palmer, Tiffany Thayer and US Air Force officials. His articles were objective, unbiased and credible.

The Pentagon should have dropped the subject right there and let poor Sid take the heat, which he was perfectly capable of doing. Instead they concocted Project Grudge, denouncing the whole business, throwing in irrelevant opinions of astronomers like Dr. J. Allen Hynek (who formulated what was to become the official anti-UFO explanation for the next 20 years) and creating a controversy that continues to this day.

## Richard Haines

*Richard Haines has worked as a NASA scientist and as a scientist at the Research Institute for Advanced Computer Science at Ames Research Center in California. He has published numerous articles and books analyzing UFO-related events. Here he describes some of the best photographic cases.*

- **Trinidad Island Photos, Atlantic Ocean, 1958, January 16, 12:15 PM.** Fortunately, one Mr. Barauna took his camera on board the ship *Almirante Saldanha*, then operated by the International Geophysical Year (IGY) for hydro-graphic ocean studies. He succeeded in taking at least four black-and-white, high-resolution photos of a craft with a domed disk against the sky with sea and/or land also in the field of view.

- **Vancouver Island, British Columbia, Canada, 1981, October 8, 11 AM.** Mr. and Mrs. D. McR. and family were on vacation when Mrs. McR. took an outstanding color 35mm photograph of a nearby mountain peak and white cloud. Later, they noticed a symmetrical domed disk in the sky. Scientific analysis of this photograph has convinced me of its authenticity. The object still cannot be identified.

- **N.E. Costa Rica, 1971, September 4, 8:25 AM.** A black-and-white high-resolution aerial photo was obtained from a government airplane flying at 10,000 feet altitude on a mapping mission. None of the flight crew saw the UFO, which was later noticed on one of the frames. Later analysis by myself and ufologist Jacques Vallee discovered that if the object were 10,000 feet from the camera, its maximum dimension would have been about 683 feet across.

## James W. Moseley

*Editor of the irreverent, gossipy insider newsletter* Saucer Smear, *James Moseley has been writing and speaking about UFOs since he co-founded the magazine* Saucer News *in 1954.*

To me, the most interesting event in 50 years of ufology was the Roswell Incident, which occurred almost at the same time as the Kenneth Arnold sighting. Whereas Arnold's sighting remains unexplained, research during the past four or five years has finally established (in my opinion) that the Roswell Incident was perhaps the greatest nonevent of the century.

When it occurred in late June or early July of 1947 (the exact date is still in dispute), the supposed Roswell Incident caused a "splash" in the national media for a few days, and then was mercifully forgotten. It wasn't until about 1978 that "witnesses" started publicly remembering stories about small alien bodies having been involved in the crash. The number of aliens and other key details differ from story to story, but True Believers are not deterred.

Over the years, the major Roswell researchers (Charles Moore, Kevin Randle, Stanton Friedman and others) have hyped their favorite witnesses while methodically discrediting others. The net result has been that all the major witnesses have now been discredited, and of course most of them are now dead. Even the crash site can't be agreed upon!

Recent research by Karl Pflock, Professor Charles Moore, and Robert Todd has shown that the crash at Roswell was almost certainly a then-classified Mogul balloon. But as the real facts have become clearer, the money-grubbing hysteria has become louder, with last year's "alien autopsy video" and now, finally, a "tell-all" book by one Colonel Philip J. Corso, Ret., who has waited a full 50 years to bring out his revelations just in time for the forthcoming Roswell Festival. Can anyone really take this seriously?

## Professor G. Cope Schellhorn

*G. Cope Schellhorn is a retired English professor, a writer, researcher and the publisher of Horus House Press near Boscobel, Wisconsin. Many Horus House books focus on UFOs and other paranormal phenomena.*

- *The successful development of SDI (Star Wars) technology, including a beam weapon capable of offensive as well as defensive uses.* Once this technology was operable and placed in orbit and in ground installations, the US military attained overwhelming tactical superiority, leading to the collapse of the Soviet regime and the true beginning of a New World Order. Now we have a new popgun technology that some evidence suggests we may be foolishly using indiscriminately against almost all ET visitors.

- *As a singular event, the January 20, 1996 crash of a UFO in Varginha, Brazil, is by far the most outstanding.* We have more than 100 witnesses to the capture of the crew. Some were netted, some shot and bagged in plastic. Despite cover-up attempts, our citizen-neighbors to the south are hard to muffle. Nevertheless, the incident has received little media attention in the US. Is the media asleep and ignorant? Or is it true that the media is controlled far more than we realize?

- *The crashes in the Southwestern US in the late 1940s and early 1950s.* Just exactly where craft came down is in dispute (Roswell? Corona? Socorro? Aztec? Elsewhere?).

The overall evidence, however, is overwhelming, even though fogged by time. But as the bard said, "murder will out" and so will truth, sooner or later.

## Antonio Huneeus

*Antonio Huneeus has been a FATE columnist for four years. He is MUFON's international coordinator, and he does international consulting and reporting on UFO topics.*

- *A good aircraft case* is one where there are multiple radar returns plus visual confirmation by pilots and ground witnesses. But the Tehran Dogfight of September 19, 1976, had much more. As a UFO cruised over Tehran's restricted airspace, two F4 Phantom jets of the Imperial Iranian Air Force were scrambled. Both aircraft experienced equipment anomalies. The dogfight's climax is described in a famous telex from the US Defense Attaché Office in Tehran. A small, brightly lit object came from the larger object and "headed straight toward the F4 at a very fast rate. The pilot attempted to fire an AIM9 missile at the object, but at that instant his weapons control panel went off and he lost all communications (UHF and Interphone)."

  Among the ground witnesses was the number three officer in the Iranian Air Force, General Nader Yousefi. A Defense Intelligence Agency evaluation concluded it was "an outstanding report. This case is a classic which meets all the criteria necessary for a valid study of the UFO phenomenon."

- *In the CE-III category*, those close encounters where occupants are also reported, I definitely have a favorite. Pirassununga is a town located in São Paulo state in Brazil. The Brazilian Air Force (FAB) estimated that as many as 500 witnesses observed the flyby and landing of a disc on the morning of February 6, 1969. The FAB UFO project SIOANI interviewed 300 of them. There were ground traces on the open field where the disc landed, and humanoids were seen levitating from the craft.

The main witness, Tiago Machado, attempted without much success to communicate with the aliens. As Machado rushed toward the humanoids, one of them shot him with a hand-held device. A beam hit his thighs and he passed out. Machado was taken to a nearby hospital and examined by a doctor; he had red spots on his thighs but was not seriously hurt. In addition, a power blackout affected Pirassununga and an important FAB Training School. All this was duly reported in the official SIOANI documents. No one has ever attempted to debunk this case.

## Cynthia Hind

*Cynthia Hind, a resident of Zimbabwe, is MUFON's Coordinator for the African Continent. She edits and publishes the biannual magazine* UFO AfriNews. *She is the author of* UFOs Over Africa.

The case that really stands out in my mind is that of 62-year-old Danie van Graan, a smalltime farmer living in Loxton, in an arid, isolated, almost desert-like area of South Africa. On the chilly, misty morning of July 31, 1975, Danie had gone to have a look at his *kraal* (animal enclosure). As Danie approached, he saw the aluminum roof of a trailer about a mile and a half away. He was surprised, but not disturbed. Government prospectors were looking for uranium in the area, and he assumed that this was their trailer.

As he drew nearer, he saw it was a rather strange trailer; more of an oval shape, with large windows and tine-like legs instead of wheels. He could see four men inside, but their movements seemed to be in slow motion.

"They were rather thin and pale," he said. "They were only about 1.5 meters [five feet] tall, and they wore cream-colored coveralls with the hoods pushed back off their heads. I could see they had fair hair, slanting eyes, and high cheekbones coming down to a pointed chin."

When Danie was about 16 feet away, the men inside suddenly looked up at him. He heard a "click," and a small flap opened on the side of the machine. Hit with a brilliant beam of light, he staggered and fought for breath as though he were drowning. He felt ill and confused and tried to get out of the light beam as quickly as he could. At the same time, the flap closed and the beam went off.

Then the machine took off very smoothly at an incredible speed, just missing the top of Danie's windmill. It disappeared within 20 seconds. As Danie staggered home, he came across his neighbor who helped him to his house and then informed the police.

When Danie took us to his *kraal* area, I saw that where the machine had stood (a six-and-a-half-foot in diameter section) the earth was hard-baked and cracked into pancake shapes; and although Danie said he had watered it well, nothing had grown there since the machine landed. The rest of the *kraal* was verdant with alfalfa.

Danie has since died. Perhaps now he will have all the answers to the enigma that puzzled him so much in the summer of 1975.

## Tatyana Syrchenko and Michail Gershtein
*Tatyana Syrchenko is editor of the Russian language* Anomaly, *a newspaper about the paranormal published in St. Petersburg, Russia; Michail Gershtein is a Russian UFO expert and correspondent.*

During the last 50 years, Soviet ufology went through uneasy times when the state censored everything connected with unidentified flying objects. It has only been since March 1989 that all interdictions have been removed and UFO reports began "gushing out" onto the pages of the state social and political publications.

In 1977, after the so-called "Petrozavodsk Phenomenon" (the launch of the satellite Kosmos-955 and possibly some real UFOs as well), the Academy of Science started its half-secret program of UFO investigations, called "Setka-AN" ("Network-AS"). Investigators sought a reliable case of contact with an extraterrestrial, and they soon found it!

Two investigators went to the town of Derzhavinsk (in Kasakhstan). Many witnesses had told of seeing a sphere of light which flew overhead like a plane before landing. They said that strange, high-speed machines moved through the steppe, following cars. The witnesses also reported contact with "strange figures" near the Pioneer children's camp Beriozka.

On the morning of June 26, 1979, the group of campers went outside the camp to play games. They suddenly noticed a bright flash on the edge of the forest. Some bright dome-shaped objects appeared there, and three figures emerged and moved toward the children. Frightened, the children turned and ran toward the camp. They reported that the creatures were 10 to 12 feet tall, with thin bodies, dressed in black clothes with bright red belts. The creatures had long arms and big spherical heads with two large eyes.

The creatures leaped at the children, following them to the camp, where many people ran out, yelling and throwing stones. The creatures stopped and then left the camp. The chief of the camp called the police and the KGB, but at first nobody came to investigate the incident. Later, investigators found 20-inch footprints and soil depressions suggesting that the creatures weighed 800-900 pounds.

Authorities were afraid of creating a panic and began spreading counter-propaganda. One official lecturer explained the incident as a "student joke."

However, investigators found many traces of some kind of vehicle on the steppe and many witnesses with similar stories. The identities of the objects and the aliens are unknown to this day.

## Giulio Brunner

*Giulio Brunner is retired from the editorship of Italy's popular magazine of the paranormal,* Il Giornale dei Misteri (The Journal of Mysteries), *published in Florence. Brunner chose to write about a pivotal Italian UFO sighting.*

In the northeastern outskirts of Florence, a large park called Campo di Marte is the site of a soccer field. It was here on October 27, 1954, a nice, tepid early afternoon, that 10,000 people witnessed an amazing event. Teams from Florence and Pistoia, a nearby town, were playing. The stadium was lit by the autumn sun, when suddenly, "I saw out of the corner of my eye somebody pointing at something in the sky," reported my friend and colleague Sergio Conti. "I looked up, too, and I saw two tiny but clearly visible flying objects of a peculiar brightness that moved quickly and crossed over the ground."

The shiny, metallic gray discs traveled on a straight line from south to north. Each had a circular "crown" of a lighter color that whirled around the axle formed by the center part of the disc, said Conti.

The two objects spent the next several minutes "playing" above the field. One object would stop, while the other sped ahead, then the other would stop and the first object would zigzag through the sky. The two objects sped north, then suddenly reversed and flew directly over the spectators. Finally, they disappeared in the south, moving at a higher speed than any known aircraft was capable of.

That same day, in other parts of town, many sightings were reported, and another odd phenomenon as well: From some of these objects a white, sticky, filament-y material similar to candy floss fell down. Professor Canneri, head of the chemistry department at Florence University, examined it and reported that it was a substance based on silicon.

*FATE Editors: These accounts and the many others that have been compiled during the past 50 years lead us to reasonably presume that UFOs are a physical reality and not just the result of single or general hallucinations, as some of those who have never seen a UFO would like us to believe.*

FATE June 1997

# About FATE Magazine

Six decades before reality TV shows and late-night radio's *Coast to Coast AM*, and countless websites, blogs, books, and movies began captivating audiences with true tales of UFOs and the paranormal – there was FATE – a first-of-its-kind publication dedicated to in-depth coverage of mysterious and unexplained phenomena.

FATE was a true journalistic pioneer, covering issues like electronic voice phenomena, cattle mutilations, life on Mars, telepathic communication with animals, and UFOs at a time when discussing such things was neither hip nor trendy. Today FATE enjoys a rare longevity achieved by only a select few US periodicals.

### Where it all began: The birth of the modern UFO era

The year was 1948. The Cold War was in its infancy, and the Space Age was still a dream…but across the nation and around the world, people observed strange objects flying through the skies.

Two Chicago-based magazine editors, Raymond A. Palmer and Curtis B. Fuller, took a close look at the public's fascination with flying saucers and saw the opportunity of a lifetime. With help from connections in the worlds of science fiction and alternative spirituality, they launched a new magazine dedicated to the objective exploration of the world's mysteries. They gave their "cosmic reporter" the name FATE.

FATE's first issue, published in Spring 1948, featured as its cover story the first-hand report of pilot Kenneth Arnold on his UFO sighting of the previous year, an event widely recognized by UFO historians as the birth of the modern UFO era.

### FATE's role in creating a new genre: The paranormal

Other topics covered in this and subsequent issues included vanished civilizations, communication with spirits, synchronicity, exotic religions, monsters and giants, out-of-place artifacts, and phenomena too bizarre for categorization. This mix of subjects set a template that the magazine would follow for six decades and counting. In many ways, FATE magazine created the genre that is now known as "the paranormal."

Palmer and Fuller's judgment of FATE's potential proved correct, and as demand for the magazine grew its publication frequency increased quickly from quarterly to bimonthly to monthly. Palmer sold his share of the magazine in the late 1950s, and Fuller brought his wife Mary aboard to help run the growing business.

FATE's success spawned scores of imitators over the years, but none lasted very long. Through the decades FATE kept going, doggedly promoting the validity of paranormal studies but unafraid to reveal major events as hoaxes or frauds when it was warranted. Among the famous cases debunked by FATE were the Philadelphia Experiment, and the book and movie versions of the Amityville Horror.

### Relevant today

So how does FATE still stay relevant after all this time? Especially in a fast-paced, high-tech world that is often short on attention span and long on cynicism, how does a magazine like FATE continue to thrive? Editor-in-Chief Phyllis Galde says, "FATE allows readers to think for themselves by providing them with stories that mainstream publications don't dare touch. The truth is, reality does not conform to the neat and tidy box that many people would like to wedge it into. Our world is a bizarre and wondrous place and our universe is filled with mystery – it is teeming with the unknown. People are longing for something more than the mundane transactions of everyday existence. FATE feeds the soul's appetite for the enigmatic, the esoteric, and the extraordinary."

### Subscribe to FATE

FATE is published in intervals throughout the year in a popular digest size. Join the family of subscribers by visiting the FATE website at www.fatemag.com.

# About Rosemary Ellen Guiley

Rosemary Ellen Guiley, executive editor of FATE magazine, is a leading expert in the metaphysical and paranormal fields, with more than 65 books published on a wide range of paranormal, UFO, cryptid, afterlife and spiritual topics, including nine single-volume encyclopedias and reference works. She has worked full-time as an investigator, researcher, author, and presenter since 1983, and spends a great deal of time in the field doing original research.

Rosemary is president and owner of Visionary Living, Inc., a publishing and media company, of which Visionary Living Publishing is a division. She makes numerous appearances on radio and in documentaries, docu-dramas and television shows.

### A personal note from Rosemary

I have been privileged to be part of the FATE family since 1991-92. Dennis Stillings, the publisher of *Artifex* magazine, brought me to the Minneapolis area to give a lecture on vampires – my book *Vampires Among Us* had just been published. In the audience were Phyllis Galde and David Godwin, editors of FATE. They invited me to contribute to FATE, and a lasting friendship was struck.

I started as a columnist for FATE; my column was called "Gateways." I joined the prestigious company of other FATE columnists and regulars, among them John A. Keel, Mark Chorvinsky, Loyd Auerbach, Antonio Huneeus, and Loren Coleman.

Over the course of time, FATE went through changes. Phyllis and David departed to set up their own publishing company, Galde Press. In the early 2000s, they purchased FATE from Llewellyn. David passed in 2012, and FATE remains under Phyllis's ownership. The economic upheavals in publishing, combined with rapid changes in the delivery of information, have impacted *FATE*. Once a monthly magazine, it is now published several times a year – still delivering the same varied and insightful content.

    I went from columnist to consulting editor, and in 2016 became Executive Editor, taking on more editing responsibilities. Phyllis and I entered into a partnership to bring you a series of books on the best from the archives of FATE on timeless topics of ongoing interest. FATE has thousands of excellent articles in its vaults, written by the best of the best, and I am pleased to make them available again.

www.ingramcontent.com/pod-product-compliance
Lightning Source LLC
Chambersburg PA
CBHW020137130526
44591CB00030B/99